KT-458-844

TWENTY-FIVE YEARS
AT BROOKLANDS TRACK
WITH THE "RAILTON ERA"

TWENTY-FIVE YEARS AT BROOKLANDS TRACK WITH THE "RAILTON ERA"

by

R. H. BEAUCHAMP,
C.Eng., M.I., Mech.E.

Regency Press (London & New York) Ltd.
125 High Holborn, London WC1V 6QA

Copyright © 1984 by R. H. Beauchamp,
C.Eng., M.I., Mech.E.

This book is copyrighted under the Berne Convention.
No portion may be reproduced by any process without
the copyright holder's written permission except for the
purposes of reviewing or criticism, as permitted under
the Copyright Act of 1956.

HERTFORDSHIRE
LIBRARY SERVICE

796.7206 842

H50 243 778 2

4 MAR 1985

ISBN 0 7212 0619 0

Printed and bound in Great Britain by
Buckland Press Ltd., Dover, Kent.

CONTENTS

Chapter   Page

1   The J. G. Parry Thomas Days, 1924-1927...   11

2   The R. A. Railton Days, 1927-1939   25

3   The War Years, 1939-1945   68

4   The Post War Years, 1945-1949   77

Finale   95

Appendix 1   98

Appendix 2   99

Dedication

To my cousin Joan Hylda Smith, whose lifetime of unfailing friendship was such a boon to me, as was her immediate family upon the dispersal of my own.

LIST OF ILLUSTRATIONS

Figure		Page
1	Map of Brooklands, works and offices	13
2	Thomas Special No. 1	18
2a	The Leyland-Thomas sprint car	21
3	Thomas Inventions Development Co. work force ...	24
4	The author	27
4a & 4b	The Napier-Railton car of Mr. John Cobb	30-31
5	The 'Brooklands' Riley Nine Team	33
6	Bluebird in 1931	36
7	Whitney Straight's Maserati	37
8 & 9	Two views of Bluebird in the T & T Workshops ...	38-39
10	The Bluebird chassis, 1932	41
11	1931 Daimler Double-Six Special	43
12 & 13	The chassis and completed car designed by R.A.R. ...	45
14	Press Day for Sir Malcolm Campbell	47
15	Gear set for Sir Malcolm Campbell's 'Blue Bird' boat ...	48
16	Complete gear box for Sir Malcolm Campbell's 'Blue Bird' boat	49
16a	Bluebird secures world record	51
17	Mr. John Cobb and Ken Taylor	54
18	Front view of the Napier-Railton	55
19	Rear view of the Napier-Railton	56
20	Mr. John Cobb in the driving seat	57
21	The car being unloaded at Utah Salt Flats	58
22	Outside its Wendover Garage	60
23	Preparing for an early trial	62
24	Press conference	64
25-28	Various Leyland Diesel Engine Adaptations ...	78-80
29	Cars for various combinations of loss of limb or limbs by drivers	82
30	The works crew and the Napier-Railton	87
31	The 'Magic Midget'	91
32	Mr. John Cobb's and Lt. Col. Gardner's Cars	93

Acknowledgement

The author and publisher would like to thank the following copyright holders for permission to use their photopgraphs: Photograph No. 6, Fox Photos Ltd.; No. 10, Sport and General Ltd.; and No. 14, The BBC Hulton Picture Library.

Foreword

I do hope the book will be popular
as we owe so much to T & T.

S. C. H. (SAMMY) DAVIS
18th November, 1980

CHAPTER ONE

The J. G. Parry Thomas Days
1924-1927

It would be as well to explain how I first became involved with being at the Track at Brooklands. At a very tender age the exciting news that a motor racing track was being opened at Weybridge was of more than passing interest. I had no idea then, of course, that seventeen years later I would be very much involved, for the following twenty-five years, with happenings at the Track and its environs.

In the meantime I had again been keenly interested, in commencing a five year training course in 1919 with the engineering firm of D. Napier & Son Ltd. of Acton Vale, in that S. F. Edge, and the Napier car he drove, had become famous for its long distance record runs at Brooklands.

In 1924, having just finished my course with the Napier Company, I noticed a situations vacant advertisement in *The Engineer* for a junior draughtsman and applied for the post. An interview that followed at Spring Gardens in London was with Mr. Ken Thomson of the Thomas Inventions Development Co. Ltd. At that time I was living with my parents at Brentford and one Sunday morning made an exploratory visit to the Track with my brother in his long-stroke Sunbeam motorcycle and sidecar. When taking a left-hand bend, the dampened front vee-block brake failed to slow the outfit and when searching for the rear foot brake this pedal apparently had disappeared! Not wishing to turn the outfit over the only object that showed some possibility of stopping us was a telegraph pole and this was struck plumb between the bike and sidecar. Hanging hard on to the right handlebar until the last second I was catapulted into the base of a hedge and woke up at home with concussion and a cracked sternum. My brother survived by pushing the front of the sidecar out with his knees. This unfortunately delayed my acceptance of the position with the Thomas Inventions Co. until I was able to buy my first 350c.c. side-valve AJS with which to journey the 17 miles each way from Brentford to Brooklands. The delay was graciously accepted by Ken Thomson via his secretary, Miss Nora James.

I was soon established in the Drawing Office the firm had at the Track. The buildings then occupied were built during the first World War for use by the RFC and were leased by the Brooklands authorities to the Thomas Inventions Development Co. They consisted of five separate buildings as shown on the sketch.

The Drawing Office was at one end of a Tyre Store used by the Dunlop Co.

This building was, I believe, used by the RFC as a photographic development section, as two zinc-covered troughs were visible, one on each side of the outer office, with a water supply which was eventually used for the development of the many blueprints made of the detail-drawings of the new racing-car project.

The office inner sanctum was occupied by Geoff Cullen who was the chief draughtsman, and a junior draughtsman called Johns and I occupied the outer office, together with the blueprint machine. We understood that the object was to provide design drawings of a completely new racing and record car which was to be powered by a 750c.c. four-cylinder engine, with an alternative 1,500c.c. straight-eight engine. My first task was to cope with details of its valve gear, and this was to follow the Leyland pattern of overhead camshaft with two-valves-per-cylinder in hemispherical heads and with the usual leaf valve springs, but without the twin cam arrangement for "positively" operating the valves as in some Leyland experimental valve gear. I believe my first contact with Parry Thomas was when busily engaged in detailing a tulip-type inlet valve, I was somewhat surprised to find a bulky figure in a Fair Isle jumper and wearing gym shoes and slacks appear by my side to see how things were going. He seemed to appear only seldom in the drawing office but his quietly spoken words were always authoritative and to the point.

The work proceeded apace. Here I should say that whilst I was with the Napier Co. (who at that time had an extremely able and talented Chief Designer in Mr. A. J. Rowledge, who was responsible for the T.75 Napier car, a competitor of the Rolls-Royce, and also the range of famous broad-arrow formation Napier "Lion" Aero engines) I was grateful to Mr. Goodwin, Bsc, and his assistant Mr. Barnes, and to Mr. Carne of the Napier Stress Section who had my

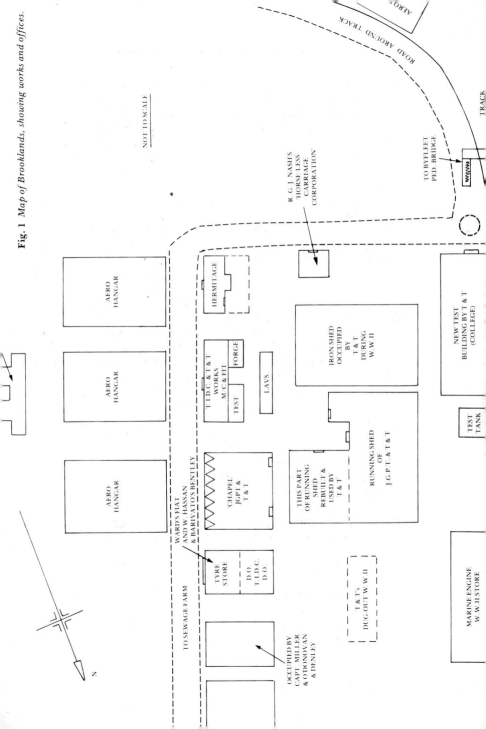

Fig. 1 *Map of Brooklands, showing works and offices.*

attention drawn closely to the importance of the theoretical side of precision engineering, when I certainly was made aware of the necessity of exact calculation of items such as the moment of inertia, modulus of section of rectangular and circular sections, leading to a most useful fundamental Data and General Formula Book built up by that Department. As I was also in close touch with the Workshops, this was a really helpful period of my engineering initiation.

Sometimes, and perhaps because of, Thomas' infrequent appearances the overall picture became somewhat disjointed. I remember it was once discovered that the camshaft was being driven at 0.66-times engine speed. Fortunately Thomas found that sufficient width had been left in the camshaft gear train to halve the width and increase the module of the driving gears and so compound them to give the correct ratio! The engine design was unusual, with a cast-iron cylinder and separate cast-iron crankcase, coupled with wet cylinder liners, and with pairs of cylinders surrounded by aluminium water-jackets. This arrangement later gave Ken Taylor, the hard-working and able man who was to build the cars, some cause for concern with the head and block gaskets. Eventually an annealed copper gasket for the cylinders, with separate reinforced rubber joints for the water-jackets, provided a satisfactory answer, although the studs with their loose sleeves operated by tommy-bar were a far from easy method of clamping the head to the block. To assist in expediting the work I recall that Ken Thomson was enlisted, in his "spare time" from his financial managerial duties, to do some work on the gearbox in the drawing office and also I believe in the progressing of work during manufacture. I understood later that he underwent a fair amount of "friendly" comment regarding the rigidity of the gearbox selector mechansim from Parry Thomas (who was a physically tough character) when in fact the drag of the Hele-Shaw type multi-plate clutch was really suspect!

There is one item of these Thomas Specials that was pure Parry Thomas and that was the design of the pistons, which logically had a truncated cone structure joining the piston head, via the gudgeon-pin bosses, to a separate skirt. In this way the compression rings were carried in a separate top land, with an oil control ring in the lower land. The explosion loads were carried directly on to the gudgeon-pins and the tapered form of the cone also assisted cooling of the piston-head by oil splash. These pistons were patterned by the

Edmore Pattern Works at Hanwell and sand cast by Miralites of Mortlake. In spite of their complicated shape I do not recall any major trouble ever being experienced with them. Incidentally, as with almost all other machined parts, they were produced in the Thomas workshops by machinists Platten, Robinson and Bryant, whose final shining product was always a delight to behold.

The engines were tested on the bench in the test shop adjoining the Workshop, (with the power being absorbed by a two-bladed external, but shrouded, air fan designed by J.G.P.T. himself), by a new recruit, Lew Motley, and it was good to hear the sound of the open exhaust whilst we were working on other details. We all had an ear cocked when the note ceased, wondering whether the stop was an involuntary one or whether some adjustment was required. But generally the testing proceeded satisfactorily. One of Motley's free time activities was to fit a spotlight to his open Austin 7, and to take pot shots at startled rabbits whilst weaving in and out of fir trees on the comparatively level ground of the Members Hill at the top of the Test Hill. His spring-frame ABC motor-cycle was a familiar sight around the works at this time, usually with his evening clothes strapped on the carrier. He was frequently seen breakfasting in the office at about ten o'clock on a grapefruit in consequence of late hours, but this was not questioned as we were all rather used to staying over the official time of a 5.30 p.m. works stop, particularly towards the end of the project, as well as appearing at the Track during such times as Easter and Whitsun Meetings, etc., in almost any useful capacity but particularly as timekeepers and pit assistants. This demonstrated the spirit of enthusiasm that Thomas and Taylor had generated throughout the works, which persisted in spite of (or because of!) Ken Thomson's vague promise of a bonus in the event of success of the venture.

Johns and I found some light relief at lunchtime in taking J.G.P.T.'s dogs Bess, an all-black Alsation, and Togo, her black and tan son, across the verge of the Aerodrome to chase rabbits that emerged from the sand-hills by the road inside the Track. It was really astonishing to see how quickly these sizeable dogs could run and twist and turn, in their frequently successful chase of young rabbits. On one occasion they both caught the same rabbit, with disastrous results for it. As the dogs were given fair quantities of fresh meat each day I imagine the exercise was good for them and it also allowed us the benefit of some fresh air across the 'drome.

When the weather was wet, an occasional diversion at lunch time was provided by Robinson allowing any interested staff to try their skill at hitting a match stick, stuck in a crack in a wall, from the other side of the shop — about 15 feet — with a pellet from his .22 Webbley air pistol. This was seldom hit, until one day when Loundes appeared and without pause knocked the match apart. This success was promptly attributed to the fact that he did not have to squint — being the only member of the firm with a glass eye, and this he seemed to agree with, with considerable glee.

Whilst we in the Drawing Office were continuing with the chassis items, the work in the Shops was being pursued on the lap-record-holding Leyland — Thomas and the Thomas Special and Marlborough (or Hooker-Thomas) engines, with Jock Pullen in charge of the Running Shed, and Lew Stone, Jack Sopp, Howard and Simmons dealing with fitting, in the main workshop. These skilful fitters also had the assistance of young apprentices and one of them, Paul Wyand, was later, after leaving us, to develop into a very solid figure to be found precariously perched on the roof of a car with a Movietone News camera at the ready, moving around the environs of the Track.

Another solid figure was Bert White, an ex-Navy Cockney, who besides being responsible for the running of the Stores was responsible for grinding and polishing cylinder heads and valve parts. The marvellous care taken with these items must have played a large part in Thomas' consistent results with his various cars in races and record bids.

I well remember one autumn night of real pea-soup fog, when all employees' cars or bikes were left at the works and Bert White headed the band of workers, joined one to the next by a long rope, across the Sewage Farm by narrow elevated tracks. This journey to the West Weybridge Station was concluded satisfactorily, although there was sometimes a bit of shunting when the leader stopped to check the route. We were all grateful for the accidents that did not happen, due to his remembered knowledge of his daily route.

At about this time, when flying at the Track was becoming increasingly popular, there was often a diversion caused by people like Dudley Watt and Joe King competing one with another in flying between the hangers. Eventually, I believe, they both succeeded separately in flying around the Track and under the Byfleet pedestrian bridge. I certainly know that Dudley Watt was successful in this, as I saw this attempt in his SE5. Quite electrifying! There was talk of flying through the hanger. Fortunately I don't think this was ever attempted but it may have been the reason why a new dope-shop was much later built outside the hanger. The dope-shop was late accidentally burnt down.

The Henderson School of Flying provided an amusing incident when one of its aspiring pilots landed successfully, after his first solo flight, but at some half a mile or so away from the Club House, with a stalled engine. Deciding that this was not the polished performance that his instructor would wish to see, and determined to taxi up to the Club House in style, he demounted to swing the propellor, but no joy — so back to increase the throttle whereupon the motor started and the conscientious pilot was chased erratically across the Aerodrome by his own plane which was finally stopped by a post and wire boundary fence.

In relation to the use of the Aerodrome by the Flying School planes, I often wondered what advance warning the pilots of these planes had of a herd of cows (sometimes accompanied by a goat) that frequently invaded the 'drome' from a nearby farm. I also wondered whether the only warning that the pilots had, could have been the obnoxious smell from the goat as it was wafted across the area. In fact the liaison between Farm and Flying School must have been pretty good, whatever its form, as I do not recall any accident of plane on cow, or cow on plane, ever occurring, or for that matter the goat ever being damaged either.

Soon after becoming involved with some minor mechanical modifications for the Flying School Chief, I was approached by one of the Flying School pupils — who was apparently having difficulty in finding a passenger to take up in his D.H. plane — after he had just acquired his 'A Class' Licence, allowing him to take a passenger up with him in this model. It was a fine day for another slant of view across the 'Drome' and Track environs, so I was pleased to accept, but was a little surprised when after a circle of the Track, we were up in a thermal from the Members Hill, and in his exuberance also up in a half loop! However there was nothing that I could do about it. I only hoped that the training the School had given him would see us safely down again. It did and we were soon bumpily taxied and stopped close to the Hangers, when I climbed stiffly and thankfully out. This was the first time ever that I was to fly and the last time at Brooklands! I was to recall this flight when later on the first parachute jump was made at the Track.

During the design development of the "flat-iron" cars there was a change in the personnel of the office staff, when Mr. A. Saunders took over the job of Chief Draughtsman from Geoff Cullen. Johns and I were both sorry to see Cullen go as he was a cheerful, bold character, as one would imagine an ex-RFC pilot to be. Whether his retirement was due to the result of World War I injuries or due to some misunderstanding with the requirements of the project I was never quite clear. But the task continued with "Pa" Saunders in charge of the Drawing Office.

Towards the autumn of 1926 the first 1,500c.c. Thomas Special was finally ready for a test run as a complete vehicle. I well remember a fine sunny day when the car was pushed up between the hangers to take advantage of a downward slope for a push start. The car was duly pushed off but all that happened was that the rear wheels locked and the car came to a standstill. Apparently one of the top bolts securing the crankcase to the chassis had been left too long and had penetrated into the timing-gear train and successfully locked it! This was soon replaced and the first run proved satisfactory.

At that time the Drawing Office was beginning to be busy again with "Babs", so that I was not in close touch with the work on the "flat-iron" cars that Ken Taylor had to undertake. But it is my impression that, apart from carburetter tuning and general adjustments, very little else was done to the car. The carburation of this car was interesting in that the car as first built obtained its air when the bulk of the supply had first passed through the sloping radiator. It can be seen from the first photograph taken of the

Fig. 2 *Thomas Special No. 1. at it's first appearance on the road outside the Thomas Inventions Development Co. Ltd. Workshops at Brooklands.*

finished car outside the works that the near side of the bonnet was not pierced for air supply to the carburetters. Later, however, the two carburetters were fed from ambient air from outside the bonnet. In October 1926, only about two years from the start of the project, the car won its first race at some 106 m.p.h.

All this I think shows the design-powers and guiding genius of Parry Thomas himself, his partner Ken Thomson, and his Chief Mechanic Ken Taylor, for their gathering of a small team together to achieve such good and effective results over such a short period of time.

Prior to 1926 the Hooker-Thomas car with its new streamlined long-tailed body and wheel discs had some successes, but very little drawing office work was done on this car, as I believe the body was built by the Gray brothers, and almost all of the tuning and running was done in the Shops by Ken Taylor, with Jock Pullen as his assistant, under the guidance technically of Parry Thomas himself.

The Leyland-Thomas cars were generally also similarly developed. The inlet to the carburetters was modified in steps, by first of all having it low down beside the radiator, and finally a higher inlet was used, trunking directly into the carburetters to take advantage of the car's forward speed and a consequent increase of pressure above atmosphere of about 1lb./sq. in. at 100 m.p.h. at the chokes, as I was later to discover.

It speaks volumes for the soundness of the original design of the Leyland-Thomas that I can only remember one engine being blown up, and this after considerable development of ignition and carburation as the bulk of the main components, apart from higher and higher compression-ratio pistons, were of original Leyland-Thomas design. Fuels were also considerably modified in conjunction with the Shell Co. with their representative "Snowy" always on hand in the paddock. It is conceivable that the small increase in pressure of the pressurised air may have been the last straw that the tubular-sections rods could not sustain! This was the "sprint" car; but the Leyland-Thomas car's performance during a six-hour record at the Track with Parry Thomas at the wheel throughout shows that in this form the car had extreme reliability. It also demonstrated the stamina and determination of J.G.P.T. himself, who was hardly able to get out of the car at the end of the record and was then laid out on the floor of the Fork timing-box and massaged back into some more limber form. His fitness from playing squash must have helped Thomas a great deal in obtaining the record. Incidentally, it was on a day of one of these record attempts that I had my first experience of driving a car. Distilled water was required in a hurry for one of the racing cars and Ken Thomson asked me to take Thomas' little sports Amilcar and collect some from the Shops and bring it out to the Track. Not wishing to tell him I had never in my life driven a car I hopped in, but had some difficulty in finding bottom gear, as there was no visible gear gate as on the Leyland-Thomas. My second-gear start wasn't elegant but the water was duly delivered. It was wanted for the Leyland during its successful attack on records up to six hours, in October, 1926, the engine having Delco ignition.

I was able myself to realise to what discomfort he must have been put when R. B. Howey was kind enough to do three laps of the Track with me as passenger in the Leyland-Thomas at about 125 m.p.h. along the Railway Straight (without a seat squab and windscreen!) to note the front wheel deflections and effect of the forward wind speed. With regard to the suspension of these cars, it is interesting to note that it was only after almost a decade or so, that many papers were written, both by members of the IAE and SAE relating to the benefits of understeer characteristics for the front-end wheel layout, whilst it would seem that Parry Thomas had anticipated these points to some degree with his leaf-spring-cum-torsion-bar front and rear suspension arrangements.

The whole of the little factory was really concerned when Thomas returned from one Track race with top-of-the-banking greenery still entangled in the offside front wheel assembly! More so, when it was learned that he had crashed the Leyland during a hill-climb at Boulogne, but had had a phenomenal escape from serious injury. My photograph shows how badly the car was damaged.

It was in 1926 that Parry Thomas was to take up the much less hazardous task of driving a bus, probably a Leyland, in London, during the General Strike. Some while later his partner Ken Thomson was to provide some light, but expensive, relief after a heavy fall of snow at the Track, in getting Faithful, a millright, to build a wooden structure across the front of the four litre Invicta, which acted as a very efficient snow plough when driven around the roads about the Works. Unfortunately, the snow built up around the radiator and his exuberant run ended in a flurry of snow and steam. His public spirited action did, however, allow the Works staff to leave that night without getting stuck in an eighteen inch drift.

J. E. P. Howey, who owned the second Leyland-Thomas, was a very popular man with all the works people. His capable handling and interchanging of cars in the Thomas stable between his friends, Thomas and Cobb, was really very able, with something of the "Three Musketeers" quality. Captain Howey's brother, R. B. Howey, was killed when his five litre Ballot crashed at Boulogne, as Thomas was to do; the Ballot was prepared for racing in Thomas' workshops. As for Thomas, I was to witness an extraordinary event when, on passing from the drawing office to the workshop one afternoon, I saw the Leyland-Thomas being driven around the Track. It was just leaving the end of the Byfleet banking at well over 100 m.p.h. when almost simultaneously a complete tyre shot over the banking and into the trees whilst a large cloud of dust emerged as the front offside wheel bit into the track. How Thomas managed to retain control and bring the car into the paddock safely was quite remarkable. I was told that his angry remarks to the Russian representative of the firm with which he was concerned on tyre testing when asked, "What is the trouble?" were a bit surprising from the son of a clergyman. It could be thought perhaps that the delicate aroma from the Russian cigarettes he sometimes smoked was really some form of apology . . .

Fig. 2A *The Leyland-Thomas sprint car in the Chapel at Brooklands after J.G.P.T. had crashed by backing into a tree, whilst attempting a Record Run at a Boulogne Hill Climb. Thomas survived with a badly bruised leg.*

These incidents caused considerable concern to his partner, Ken Thomson, and all his work-people, who realised the irreplaceable value of Thomas to the TID Co. This was also especially so with the drawing office staff who were now engaged in producing the working drawings necessary to modify the Higham Special—once the property of Count Zborowski—into a vehicle with which Thomas had set his heart on taking the World's Land Speed Record. (The car was eventually to be named "Babs", after his niece Barbara, who was an occasional visitor to the Track, together with the Duke-Williams family, and for these younger members a donkey was stabled at the Track by Thomas for their pleasure. This donkey lived, in fact, in the original wooden shed—later replaced by the T & T brick, steel-girder, glass and asbestos-roofed building—used by Thomas as a "running shed" (see plan) where it kept Tommy Hann's ancient racing Lanchester "Softly Catchee Monkey" company.) Thomas realised that this would entail producing a vehicle with a high power-to-weight ratio for the best possible acceleration up to its maximum speed and for this reason the overall weight was kept to a minimum. The existing heavy cross-drive and gearbox items were retained in the "towards-the-rear" position, as this was an aid to adhesion. Considerable work was done in the Shops to produce effective carburation and progressive throttle control. All this effort resulted in records at the Track and in 1926 the Land Speed Record was successfully raised to 169.23 m.p.h. at Pendine.

Almost all the successful races and records won by Parry Thomas were backed very efficiently by the wonderful experimental work done by the Dunlop Co. in producing the tyres required and also by the always-cheerful and hard-working "Dunlop" Mac and his assistants who on long distance records could sometimes hardly be seen behind stacks of tyres. On the subject of wheels and tyres some controversy was aroused by Thomas fitting wheel discs to the Hooker-Thomas and Leyland-Thomas in sprint car form, but I remember some 30 years later that in windless ambient conditions a car with the then-standard wheel discs, running in conditions of ice, was found to have its discs coated on the outside with radial ice spikes in the form of a star closely following the shape of the disc, which seemed to prove that Thomas was right in that the separation of the airflow from one side of the wheel to the other had no deleterious effect on the wheel rotation.

Later on in the year "Babs" was transported again to Pendine and Thomas put his own World Land Speed Record up to 171.09 m.p.h. In 1927 Malcolm Campbell was to break this by achieving a speed of 174.88 m.p.h. in his Napier-Campbell, with the well-developed Napier "Lion" aero-engine. After the successful run of 1926, Thomas and Taylor had been busy in the works extracting more horse-power from the Liberty engine of "Babs" and in March 1927 Thomas again took the car to Pendine in a determined effort to better Campbell's record. This effort, unfortunately, ended in disaster, and Thomas was killed. The exact cause or sequence of events that led to the horrific crash and to Parry Thomas' death will probably never be exactly established, but the whole of the Thomas Inventions Development Co. and hosts of his friends were to mourn the passing of a brave and courageous man of very great talent.

The whole works appeared quite dazed for several days, with the dogs wandering around, with lowered heads. (Bess and Togo were cared for eventually by a friend of Thomas, George Duller, the well-known jockey and racing driver, and his wife.) The tuning side of the business had been expanding, but in an effort to remain a viable business the drawing office had been vacated and one room in "The Hermitage" occupied by myself, with the blueprint machine across the corridor in the bathroom. This was in order that work in the drawing office could continue on an aero-engine that Thomas was developing whilst the work on "Babs" was continuing in the Shops at the same time. This aero-engine was to be of about 30-litres (presumably eventually for "Babs") with two eight-cylinder blocks in the form of a Vee and with single sleeve-valves operated by cranks from below the level of the crankshaft. A model of this gear and copious charts of valve timing and porting had already been concluded, but I was still working on this when Ken Thomson reformed the company by taking Ken Taylor into the newly-titled firm of Thomson & Taylor (Brooklands) Ltd. as his Co-Director.

I was to learn much later that Parry Thomas and Ken Thomson (who was of a New Zealand family from the North Island at Rotorua, and who finished his career in the Army with the rank of Major) met soon after the end of World War I and were both concerned in the design by J.G.P.T. of a mechanical-cum-electrical transmission for the Australian Railways. They were to meet again in this country after Thomas had built and exhibited the Leyland straight-eight

Fig. 3 *Thomas Inventions Development Co. Work Force, taken soon after the death of J. G. Parry Thomas. The group was taken outside the Brooklands Workshop.*
Front row, left to right: *Lownds, Pugh, 'George', Paul Wyand, Carter, unknown.*
Second row: *Taylor-DO, Duke Williams, Ken Taylor (GHKJT), Ken Thomson (KJT), with Togo, 'Pa' Saunders, R. H. Beauchamp, Johns-DO, Robson.*
Back two rows: *Jock Pullen, Bert White, Smith, three names not recollected, Joe Stone, Robinson, Jack Sopp, Simmons, Bryant 'Bungy', Platten, Howard.*

luxury car at Olympia in the early 1920s. This car certainly created a sensation at the Motor Show, but after only eight were sold the project was stopped, as I believe the then Leyland Chief—Henry Spurrier, senior—felt that the truck and bus business could not support its continued building.

Parry Thomas and Ken Thomson then formed the Thomas Inventions Development Co. Ken Thomson's brother Hedley had been concerned with the Hooker Co., especially on the development of a gauged "Newall" type system of limits for use in precision engineering, and now that Thomas had the only two remaining Leyland cars unsold, together with many gauges from the Leyland Co. The Thomas Invention Development Co. was soon established at Brooklands with my involvement in its activities under the design guidance of Parry Thomas—who was the second of a number of highly-qualified and gifted mechanical and electrical engineers with whom I have been fortunate to be associated, then and later, throughout my career.

CHAPTER TWO

The
R. A. Railton Days
1927-1939

It was not long after the formation of Thomson & Taylor (Brooklands) Ltd. that the position of Chief Designer was filled by Mr. Reid A. Railton. He was a BSc from Rugby and Manchester University who was beginning to produce the Arab car in small numbers at Letchworth. Upon my introduction to him, we soon found a very good understanding that was to last for the following twelve years, and intermittently over the next half a century.

His first remarks, however, were not particularly encouraging, as when I explained that I was working on the sleeve-valve aero-engine project that Parry Thomas had started, he immediately said, "Well we are going to stop that." This certainly showed a direct approach but I was soon pleased to hear that we were to start work on a special car for John Cobb, which would be powered by a similar Napier Lion engine to that which I had been involved with in its type testing days with the Napier Co. Apparently John Cobb was not satisfied with the performance of his V12 Delage and a new car was to be built from scratch to improve his Brooklands performances, as well as for long distance records. This was marvellous news, and with the engine-drawings available, work was soon started on the proposed layout as outlined by Mr. Railton.

Unfortunately, in the same way that I had a motorcycle accident when starting with the Thomas Inventions Co., I managed to have another more serious one soon after starting with Thomson & Taylor. It might be as well to mention here that when a sparrow flies into one's front wheel this should not provide a good reason for looking backwards to see if it is dead, as even at forty miles per hour, a lot of distance is covered, and B-class roads are seldom straight for long. In short, my footrest-scraping slide failed to keep me out of the rear wheel of a now stationary car around the bend, and the resulting somersault gave me a compound leg fracture that kept me immobile for six months. Once again, however, Ken Thomson, who kindly took time off from his many duties to visit me, agreed with Mr. Railton that the job would be kept open for me as soon as I felt fit to return. In the meantime "Pa" Saunders was maintaining progress with the work and I returned to find that the drawing office was now occupying an end room in "The Hermitage", nearest to the workshop with Mr. Railton's office at the same end of the building.

This car was an absorbingly interesting vehicle to work on, in all its aspects. As the weeks rolled by the objective manner in which Mr. Railton tackled all the problems involved was a revelation. The necessarily long wheelbase, due to the size of the Napier engine, was of advantage in the car's later task of riding the notorious Brooklands bumps. It would be as well here to enlarge a little on this remark about the "notorious Brooklands bumps". One must remember that the Track was first opened in 1907, only as a result of the generous and unselfish determination of Mr. H. F. Locke King, whilst the Napier Railton car, as it became to be known, did not begin to circulate around the Track until twenty-six years afterwards. During this time the Brooklands authorities, did very useful annual winter work on repairing damaged sections, but the main bump at the transition of the Home banking and the Railway straight was not such an easy problem to dispose of. The reason being that at this point the Track ran over the River Wey and was supported on a wooden pile structure which over the years had settled to a larger degree than the earth supported Home banking. It says much for the skill of Mr. Railton as a car designer and also of the skill of Mr. John Cobb as a car driver that the resulting leap into the air at this point of the Track during many a race and record run was accepted as inevitable.

It was obvious from Dame Ethel Locke King's occasional presence at the Track, mostly during the sunny days of autumn when the Track was closed, that she supported her husband in his efforts to make the Track a success. This elegant lady, in tweeds, could

Fig. 4 *The Author at work in the Thomson & Taylor (Brooklands) Ltd. Drawing Office—'The Hermitage' at Brooklands.*

sometimes be seen looking over the estate, together with a stalwart retainer and sometimes with a hoe, which in view of the size of the estate was enlightening.

Reverting to the Napier Railton car, the underslung frame at each end and its additional check straps above each axle allowed much more than the usual axle movements. A great deal of attention was given to the suspension, the duplicated main leaves of both front and rear springs being also comparatively wide in order to absorb the high engine torque involved, and with rebound rubbers on the frame, together with hand adjustable Telecontrol and pre-set shock absorbers, completed an assembly that was to perform very satisfactorily. The vertical movement of the front axle was also controlled by a tie-rod under each front spring, giving a "Watts type" movement to the axle, which together with a long drag link from the adapted Bentley steering-box ensured the least feed-back to the steering wheel, with consequent benefits to the steering of the car. The good old Napier engine was isolated from any wracking from the main frame by a three-point-mounted sub-frame and the airscrew shaft was modified to take a very large-diameter, machined-all-over flywheel to house a single-plate clutch. This arrangement served two main purposes in that it provided a good flywheel effect for the engine — now that no propeller effect would occur — during gear changes, and the single-plate clutch would ensure that there was no clutch drag to interfere with the small crash-type gearbox during gear changes, and so safeguard it.

Suffice it to say that throughout the work high quality materials were used, in a serious effort to keep the overall weight down to a minimum.

During the manufacture and construction of the car the close co-operation of Ken Taylor was most helpful, and I well remember his remark that there was no real point in limiting a bolt's clearance hole to $\frac{1}{64}''$ when $\frac{1}{32}''$ was just as effective from a clamping point of view. This "clamping effect of clearance bolts" comment of his was later to lead to torque tightness testing for special applications throughout the range of bolt sizes. He also suggested that where a ring of studs was required to be fitted, they should have pin-faced seats for a washer and castle nuts, the nuts being wired together for total security, such was his meticulous attention to detail. P.T., as he was called by Mr. Railton (to distinguish this "Ken" Taylor from "Ken" Thomson), was also helpful, during the eventual running of the car, in tailoring a solid footrest to safeguard John Cobb's left foot from the open-running clutch mechanism, and to assist him in bracing himself in the driving seat. A firmly-anchored armchair seat, closely fitting his hips as a lateral anchor, was also fitted. Before taking the car to Utah brackets were added at the front frame end for a quickly-detachable set of headlamps to be either added or demounted according as to whether the car was running during daylight or night-time hours. Another item schemed for the American runs was a 100-gallon fuel tank with its Bentley type quick filler. Saunders, a kindly man and a good engineer, had now left the firm to take up a position with the Vauxhall Co. and an Italian friend of Mr. Railton in the cheerful personage of Achille Sampietro had now joined the drawing office staff. Not surprisingly, being confronted with and solving all the problems connected with these high speed cars, Mr. Railton's health was often troubled with migraine headaches and it was during one of a number of visits to the Alpine area to recuperate—this time in Italy—that Mr. Railton I believe first met Sampietro. R.A.R. once asked him to check the capacity of the tank already drawn up—with the rapid use of his calculus method "Sammy" reported 102 gallons. I insisted on 100 gallons and I could see by the twinkle in R.A.R.'s eye that he agreed that—each in his own way—we were both right Sammy from a theoretical angle and myself from a practical angle. On another occasion he asked us what would be the diameter of a steering column, given certain conditions of load for a light alloy tube of 10 s.w. gauge. Sammy said 2″ dia. and more for fun than any other reason I suggested $2\frac{1}{8}''$ dia. Here again R.A.R. seemed amused as on this occasion Sammy was correct from a practical angle whereas my result could be considered more correct—this time from a theoretical angle—as these odd diameters were not readily obtainable at the time. On other reliability grounds the scheme was not used anyway, but this is just mentioned to illustrate the many considerations given for just one other small design item.

It was about this time that the scheme of adding a starting gear (with an R.A.R.-Lucas motor) to the car was undertaken by J. B. Perrett who had joined the firm in 1934. As the motor in the disengaged position lay between the two forward sections of the near side rear springs—I was somewhat anxious in the layout to ensure that the motor did not get knocked off on the bumps.

Later again another very ingenious scheme of a vertical aerofoil was mounted at the front end of the car, balanced by an arm with a ball filled with lead shot (as on some light-fittings used about then), the purpose of which was to provide an inward component of effort at the front end to take some of the strain off the driver in continuously circling a 12-mile diameter circle at record speed.

A further exercise in the theory of reverse entropy was found to be necessary, when, due to the continuous running, the oil temperature in the rear axle was found to be mounting dangerously. The addition of a ribbed light alloy sump, suitably attached to the steel, machined all over, rear axle gear casing and so positioned into the air stream under the car as to abstract the heat generated by the main bevels and differential gears, was a very successful solution to the problem.

Fig. 4A *The Napier-Railton Car of Mr. John Cobb in its Brookland Track form ready for its first test run. Besides many long distance records in America at Bonneville Salt Flats, and also at Brooklands, the Car also holds the Brooklands Track Record, when driven by John Cobb himself.*

Fig. 4B *These two views of the long distance Napier-Railton car show the complicated exhaust system required to satisfy the Brooklands Automobile Racing Club Regulations and* race track ready.

From some notes I have dated January 1935 this car speed could be 160 m.p.h. with an effective rear wheel circumference of 128.5″, and rear axle ratio of 1.68-1 at 2,200 r.p.m. but there was no governor on the engine speed — so the car's maximum speed was not assessed — and was presumably arranged by mutual consent with the chef d'equipe, usually Mr. Railton, John Cobb needing no persuading to put his foot down, and the basic capabilities of the engine to exceed the above speed became well known later.

This car was eminently suitable for these long-distance records, as after hours of pounding, the Bonneville, Utah salt surface tended to break up resembling an even worse track than that at Brooklands. It also says much for the strength and stamina of John Cobb himself, as well as that of his equally tough and cheerful co-driver Charles Brackenbury who assisted him.

In the late 1920's whilst the work on the Napier-Railton was going on, R.A.R. had been working on the Riley Nine chassis and by verbal instructions to mechanics had cut and re-welded an existing Riley frame to provide the first of a range of Brooklands-type Riley cars that were to become well known. This first particular chassis with shortened wheelbase and the centre section swept out to the full width of the car enabled the driver to sit to one side of the propeller shaft, in very close proximity to the ground. The engine was also considerably modified and great interest was aroused when, on its first outing, a maximum speed of 103 m.p.h. was attained when driven by Mr. Railton himself. This was a notable performance for a 1,100c.c. car and ensured the continued support of Mr. Victor Riley.

Some trouble was experienced and conquered with the running clearance of the new pistons and all the Ulster TT cars were equipped with a special large sized ribbed aluminium alloy oil sump complete with a vertical stem and quick filler lid. The rockers and their push-rods also caused some concern regarding material selection for wear, as although this tended to be compensated for by valve stretch, the valve timing could be affected. The water circulation was therefore carefully considered.

This design and development work led to the arrangement and marketing of two stages of tune that any private owner could purchase for the improved running of the now famous Riley Nine.

During this time of preparation T & T's had acquired a small Heenan and Froude water-type power brake on which test-bench all the Riley engines were run. As the water pressure was variable — and sometimes non-existent! — P.T. soon had installed a roof-high cistern for its use. We were now in what I suppose could be called "limited production" with these modified Riley engines and perhaps because of my previous experiences of this brake I was co-opted into the test shop to help with the work. I arrived in the test shop one morning to see an engine ready for test on a trolley but no assistance around, and not wishing to delay the test hoisted it on to the bench. Unfortunately this resulted in a ruptured groin muscle, and I was not long in receiving good medical attention in the local Brentford Cottage Hospital at P.T.'s suggestion.

Back again after a month away my moral was almost immediately raised by the sight of the Maina & Villiers designed Blue Bird Land Speed Record car of Malcolm Campbell standing outside the workshop with its brilliant blue and yellow paintwork shining in the sun. Here obviously was the start of another very interesting project and I can perhaps best quote from an extract of a paper by Mr. Railton entitled "Blue Bird 1930-33" written for the Institution of Automobile Engineers Proceedings Vol. 28 Session 1933-34:

Fig. 5 *The 'Brooklands' Riley Nine Team prepared by T & T for the first Ulster Tourist Trophy Race, lined up at Brooklands Track, shortly before they left for Ireland.*

"The first Napier-engined Blue Bird was built in 1926 to the designs of Mr. J. Maina and Mr. A. Villiers, and its original engine was of 450 h.p.

"To account for the form and general design of the car as it is today, it may be of interest to recount the position when the author first took the job in hand in 1930. The previous year Campbell had taken his old Blue Bird car to South Africa and had put up an average speed of 218 m.p.h. over the mile. Unfortunately for him, Segrave was at Daytona with the Golden Arrow at the same time, and had put the record up to 231 m.p.h. — a figure which Campbell's car was quite unable to reach. The Blue Bird, as it then was, had a Napier engine giving just over 900 h.p. with a clutch and transmission disposed in the ordinary manner. The driver sat over the propeller tube on the centre line of the car, and the body was streamlined as well as was possible with the necessarily high driving position. The radiator was very small and was carried in the nose of the car, the exit for the air behind the radiator being through a gap in the undershield.

"Early in the new year of 1930, Campbell made up his mind to make an attempt on Segrave's record of 231 m.p.h. He had in mind the use of the supercharged Napier racing engine which had been developed for seaplanes in connection with the Schneider Trophy, and at this point he got into touch with the author to advise him on the feasibility of rebuilding the old car with this new engine.

"Obviously, given the time and the money, the best course would have been to have built a completely new car round the new 1,400 h.p. Napier engine, and this, of course, is what we should have preferred to do. However, the money was limited, and Campbell was determined to go to Daytona the following January, so the task immediately resolved itself into that of rebuilding the existing car. In the end, the only major units of the old car that survived were the front axle and brake gear, the steering gear and the frame side members; but the resulting saving of time made it just possible for the car to be ready for the appointed date."

The challenge now was not to beat Thomas' 171 m.p.h. but to break the ⋅231.44 m.p.h. record that Segrave held and the time available was just one year, with a car to be modified that had previously not exceeded 206 m.p.h. A start was soon made on a 1/8-scale layout with the new supercharged Napier Lion engine and the existing frame with a new clutch and gearbox with the layshaft offset 7″, driving the offset rear axle through the propellor shaft and tube which was now alongside the driver. From this preliminary layout a wooden-based 1/10-scale model was made, with all the major units in wood and gauze simulation for the new radiator added, smoothly clothed in plasticine to achieve a streamlined form. This particular scale was chosen to allow the Vickers wind-tunnel results to be quickly transposed into full-scale form, and news of the results achieved from R.A.R. were good, in that we were to go ahead with the project as he had planned. A Mr. Plumb was enlisted to deal with the rear axle scheme and details whilst I tackled the forward section, and soon we were issuing drawings of structural parts, hand forging drawings, and casting details. The production of parts was marvellously assisted by such outside firms as John Thompson, Firth Derihon, David Brown, ENV, and many others at a later date. We were now working in the British inch system of measurement, as against the metric system of Parry-Thomas, and as my training was concerned with inches I fell back into the use of the standard "Newall" System. Mr. Railton with P.T. soon agreed that some of these limits were too close for the job in hand and himself considered how most running-fits could be modified to give an equivalent of about 10,000 miles of running of an ordinary vehicle, to avoid catch ups. In a similar way the Hoffman Bearing Co. supplied bearings of "000"-type indicating a "free" clearance greater than normal practice would require, upon examination of the application in question.

Very little trouble was experienced with the car abroad, with the exception of a tendency for the gearbox dogs to kick-back if the gear change was not exactly timed. As usual the Dunlop tyres performed faultlessly and both runs were completed without stopping.

The following year the car was again taken to Daytona after modifications to the radiator size and its cowling and again broke the World Land Speed record on February 24th, 1932 with a speed of 253.97 m.p.h.

In the meantime there was plenty of interest in customers' cars, and the office planimeter and pipette were kept busy checking compression ratios with the workshop milling machine machining cylinder heads, as well as design modifications of most items for the top end of an engine or the front end or tail of a car. All to the same

end of either improved speed or acceleration, suspension or road-holding and handling, but seldom having comfort predominantly in mind! There was for instance the ingenious internal gear for the blower drive of Whitney Straight's Maserati (which not only increased the blower speed in relation to the engine but also positioned the blower correctly between the front cross member and the engine) as well as steering modifications made for him to this car. With these modifications, Straight successfully took the Brooklands Mountain Circuit lap record at some 78 m.p.h., a speed that was not equalled at that time by any other car irrespective of engine size, with a "D" Class car of under three-litres, which certainly showed his skill and daring as a first class driver.

Great assistance was given by a small local firm of gear cutters — Sykes of Staines — who supplied form cutters for this blower drive and even took some time and trouble to sort out suitable cutters for the gears of S. C. H. Davis' ancient Leon Bollee three-wheeler, albeit a gear which resulted in somewhat increased backlash clearance which was however admissible!

Fig. 7 *Whitney Straight's Brooklands Mountain Circuit lap record Maserati car in the Paddock at Brooklands.*

Fig. 6 Opposite *Bluebird in its 1931 form on display in Roxted Showrooms after its return to this country, after successfully raising the LSR at Daytona to 246.09 m.p.h. almost exactly a year after the scheme was first launched.*

Figs. 8 & 9 *Two views of Sir Malcolm Cambell's 'Bluebird' in the T & T Workshops with Reid Railton discussing a point with Ken Taylor, while Simmons and Reading are working on the car's brake gear, in one case assisted by a Dewandre representative.*

The ill-fated Bentley of Sir H. Birkin was also fitted with an instrument panel bulkhead that decided the line of the new single-seater body and with positive displacement blower modifications and silencer details to comply with the regulations then in force, these items enabled him at one time to take the Brooklands lap record.

In April 1932 Malcolm Campbell presented Mr. Railton with a drawing of the Rolls-Royce "R" engine with the suggestion that this engine should now power the Blue Bird! A new frame would be required due to the length of the R-R engine. As the R-R engine torque was almost double that of the Napier the whole transmission had to be rechecked and eventually a new clutch, layshaft, propeller shaft and rear axle bevels were schemed, detailed, and produced together with modified shock-absorbers and road springs, with again a revised radiator, mounting and cowling. The materials were all carefully checked as the relevant parts had to be encased in the existing gearbox and axle casing which R.A.R. had decided must be used again if the record was to be taken in the following February. Eventually the car was made ready in the time available and the record was taken, after the mechanics had made a modification in double quick time in America to an oil seal scroll at the gearbox output shaft end. The speed recorded was 272.46 m.p.h.

In the interim period another interesting car to evolve was the engineering involved in placing the 4-litre Sunbeam V12 roller-bearing engine in a new chassis with a Wilson s.c. epicyclic gear-box. New suspension and some very large composite brake drums of light alloy and carbon steel were also fitted and with a new body the car successfully took the class C lap record for the Mountain circuit the same year.

During the late 1920s and early 1930s the works and design office had the unique experience of having dealings with a remarkable range of cars including Alfa Romeo, Amilcar, Bentley, Bugatti, Daimler, Delage, Duesenberg, Fiat, Hornet, Invicta, Leyland 8s, MG Magnette and Midget, Maserati, Morris, Riley, Thomas Specials, Salmson, Talbot and Triumph. This list may not be complete but it is sufficient to show what a wonderful chance it gave to see how various designers tackled similar problems.

Fig. 10 Opposite *The photograph is of the 'Bluebird' chassis, taken towards the end of 1932, before the body was fitted, before its eventual successful record run in February of the following year.*

Most of these cars were used by their owners for races and records on the Track, which meant that in addition to the tuning work carried out in the T & T Workshops, an additional task was necessary in that all cars using the Track had to be fitted with an exhaust system that satisfied the Silencer Regulations of the Brooklands Automobile Racing Club (B.A.R.C.). These Regulations (see Appendix 2) were instituted after World War I in around 1920 as a result of complaints of noise from the inhabitants of houses in the near vicinity of the Track.

This was a recurring complaint — probably instituted originally by the noise from the open exhaust of aero engined cars of the type of Count Zborowski's Chitty Bang Bangs, Ward's Fiat, Chassagne's Sunbeam, Campbell's Vieux, Charles Trois and others.

The exhaust systems required by these Regulations caused the D.O. some anxiety, as even if the Regulations could be completely satisfied dimensionally, the passing judgement was in the hands of the Club Scrutineers, who had the final word as to whether or not the car could be allowed on to the Track.

I remember the fact that small holes allowed in the fish tail surfaces was not taken advantage of, as this would have been a time consuming effort, and did not help to minimise noise, as unless the fish tail ends were double folded, ferruled and bolted on the larger models, the resulting noise from vibration of the fish tails could be even louder than that from an open exhaust!

The bracketry to support these systems could also be something of a headache, but I do not recall any serious failures of them.

The pictures of the Napier-Railton shown indicates probably the most complicated system of exhaust bracketry we ever produced, when in view of the fact that each of the three banks of cylinders approached eight litres, it was not surprising that R.A.R. gave the scheme his personal attention.

It was in 1930 that Mr. Railton, in consultation with Mr. Simpson (who was at that time Chief Designer of the Daimler Co.) accepted the brief of designing a low-slung touring car to be built by the Daimler Co. from their mainly existing "standard" components. I was given the task of producing the necessary working drawings with good assistance from another Daimler man in their drawing office at Coventry. I was now the enthusiastic owner of a long-stroke Sunbeam motorcycle and this was used to commute between Brentford and

Fig. 11 *1931 Daimler Double-Six Special with lowered chassis engineered by Reid Railton in co-operation with the Daimler Co. with 1974 Series Two Daimler Double-Six 2-door in the background.*

Coventry or Brooklands, at week-ends. A friendly rivalry between a Coventry man who visited Putney using an o.h.v. Rudge bike often resulted in this inter-city 100 miles or more run being made in something like 2 hr. 10 min. The car used a standard Daimler radiator for a Double-Six Daimler sleeve-valve engine, clutch and crash box with a short propeller shaft driving a worm drive rear axle—with these components in a new low-slung frame. A large petrol tank at the rear together with two spare wheels aft of this and a Gurney Nutting touring body resulted in the whole assembly being a rather splendid touring car. The work was completed in six months and the first chassis was delivered to its owner, a certain Capt. Wilson, in 1931. I was grateful for the fine co-operation of the Daimler Co. and found it a very pleasant project to work on.

1934 was a particularly interesting year as two projects of widely differing characteristics were pursued. The first was of a chassis to take the Riley engine developed by Raymond Mays and his colleague Peter Berthon and this was to be suitable for Grand Prix type races such as the Mountain Circuit. In consequence it was vitally necessary to provide a chassis with a minimum weight and maximum torsional rigidity as well as having an efficient braking system. A layout was made posing the question of an over- or under-slung rear end which could have had a hypoid or a worm drive axle to achieve a low single seating position for the driver over the propeller shaft. This was soon discarded by R.A.R. who was not unaware of the fact that the serious accident that S. C. H. Davis had had with an Invicta car was partly due to the centre of gravity of the car being at about hub height, and which on a bad surface—adhesion wise—could and did give an instantaneous break away, impossible to correct. The ERA, as it was to become, therefore was designed with a much cheaper and more tribologically efficient composite light alloy casing and steel trumpeted rear axle of a straight-tooth bevel type. With this arrangement with a comparatively high centre of gravity, the driver had some "feel" of the gravitational effects on a bend, and with the "balloon" tyres R.A.R. suggested, then fitted to a GP car for the first time, also had the benefit of a contact "patch" of increased area.

Before the work on the ERA cars was really complete the determination of Malcolm Campbell was again in evidence, in that he was keen to break the Land Speed Record by being the first to achieve 300 m.p.h. Mr. Railton had previously been dissatisfied with

Figs. 12 and 13 *The photograph 12 shows the first chassis, designed by R.A.R. as it was rolled out of T & T's Workshop, after being built there. The following photograph 13 shows a completed car by the T & T Running Shop, and this successful project evolved as a result of the initial work and enthusiasm of Mr. Raymond Mays and Peter Berthon on the development of the Riley engine, with co-operation of original chassis built by T & T and also invaluable sponsorship from Mr. Humphrey Cook in the formation of the firm of English Racing Automobiles.*

the fairing of the R-R engine into the windscreen and tail as well as the frontal car aspects. It was found that with a new body entirely, the projected frontal area could be somewhat reduced which together with a smoother surface area resulted in much better drag figures.

A new honeycomb flat radiator, almost the full width of the car, was mounted at the front end, taking its air entry from a slot across the front end, and exiting just in front of the front wheels above the nose fairing. This air entry slot was fitted with a shutter operable by the driver, which he was to close with a separate lever just before the car entered the mile timed section, and the effect was to reduce the air drag through the radiator as well as to avoid "warmed" air entering the air duct entry to the engine. Just aft of the twin rear wheels, now to be fitted, were two air brakes—one on each side of the car in the top skin of the body of two square feet area each. These flaps were mounted on a tube inside the body and operated to an angular position by a lever on the tube and powered by a large cylinder—vacuum operated. The adhesion of the twin rear wheels was met by the addition of some 1,500lb. of lead, 800lb. of which was arranged to be fairly easily demountable. These two questions of adhesion and braking were carefully gone into by R.A.R. as it was becoming increasingly difficult to be asured of a sufficiently good and long track at Daytona to achieve the speed required. The driver controls all needed fairly considerable effort. The steering, with a road wheel movement of a maximum of 10° from the straight ahead position, was now equipped with a TTN Products inertia damper, the front axle movement being severely restricted by six friction shock-absorbers, one pair operating from the top of the kingpins for maximum effect. The clutch had a long movement with about 70lb. on the pedal and the accelerator pedal movement was also fairly long as in addition to operating long semi-flexible controls to the engine a further travel was required to trigger off the vacuum operation for the air brakes. The wheel brakes themselves were vacuum servo controlled. The car was again taken to Daytona and in March 1935

Fig. 14 Opposite *Press Day for Sir Malcolm Campbell with his latest 'Blue Bird' Rolls Royce car in the Paddock at Brooklands, having just left T & T's Workshops en route for America. His son Donald may be seen in the picture, in his school cap, just south of the right hand front wheel.*

achieved a record speed of 276.82 m.p.h. The conditions under which this record was taken were far from ideal, and later in the year the information regarding the possibility of the Salt Flats at Bonneville, Utah was looked at, as not only was Campbell troubled by the uneven track but the sand particles were a painful hazard. Mr. Railton was convinced that the car could exceed the 300 m.p.h. that Campbell had set his heart on and the following September the car was taken to Utah and his and Campbell's expectations were realised when the record was broken at 301.13 m.p.h.

It was in September 1936 that my notes indicate that that an increasing gear for Sir Malcolm Campbell with its support and drive tube from the engine weighed separately gave a total of 283lb. This statement seems to indicate that early in that year (and it must have been almost immediately after attaining his 1935 Land Speed Record) Sir Malcolm was in touch with the Vosper Co. to produce a boat for him for an attack on the water speed record. The machinery was to be designed by Reid Railton, and in this field he was again to show great ingenuity. The normal procedure at that time was to couple the converging lines (in side view) of the input drive shaft and the output propeller shaft by an angled pair of bevel gears, with

Fig. 15 *Gear set. Sir Malcolm Campbell's 'Blue Bird' boat. Produced by David Brown & Co. Ltd. to the design of Mr. Railton for the world water speed record.*

resultant complication of thrust forces through the box and on to the box supports. R.A.R.'s solution was to produce a tubular shaft drive from the engine, driving through a dog clutch and a pair of helical spur gears, through an internally cut pair of straight-tooth bevel wheels, not only to give the required angle of drive to the propeller shaft but also to offset its forward thrust, with bearings contained in a steel housing, the residual thrust from the propeller being taken

Fig. 16 *Complete gear box. Sir Malcolm Campbell's 'Blue Bird' boat. Designed by R.A.R. and built by T & T.*

through the light alloy box casing on to a composite cross-member in the boat. The gear set was produced by David Brown of Huddersfield.

The boat itself duly arrived at Brooklands (by road) and was slung up on the wooden lattice supported roof beams of the Chapel at two attitudes to establish the exact centre of gravity, with some anxiety. The machinery with a walking stick control to the dog clutch, the two side guiding keels, rudder with its Arens control, an inlet trunking and instruments including pitot tube all fitted, with the presence of Leo Villa, Sir Malcolm's mechanic, much in evidence.

In addition, one of the most noteworthy and essential items was the semi-circular and tapering form of the steel water pick-up tube at the rear of the boat together with its supports which functioned perfectly.

I believe it was Leo Villa who related an incident that he witnessed during one of the first trials that took place before the record was taken. As previously mentioned, the boat's engine power was transmitted through a dog clutch operated by the driver, when all was ready for a run. The reason for a dog clutch being used was the fact that weight saving on the hull was a prime consideration, as any excess weight would mean that a longer run would be required and so increase the danger of running into driftwood. On this particular run, R.A.R. was amongst the personnel on the wooden floating pontoon from which the boat was to start. With the engine running at its usual high speed tick over and the dog clutch being engaged, the volume of water moved by the 14″ diameter propellor turning instantaneously at some 3,000 r.p.m. was both surprising and rock making of the pontoon. As the boat sped off in a cloud of spray, it was seen that R.A.R. bowed and doffed his trilby hat at the fast disappearing Sir Malcolm and boat, who was possibly quite oblivious to the swell he had caused.

It is interesting to reflect that the power from the Napier Engines of Mr. John Cobb's L.S. Record car (which design was started almost a year later) also used a mechanical coupling in lieu of the more usual friction clutch (although in that case it was of a more sophisticated design being of a lockable roller type free wheel) but the reason for its use was similar in both cases, i.e. to save both space and weight in the coupling and its control.

The boat record was duly taken at 141.74 m.p.h.

Reverting to the earlier 1930s, a number of different projects were presented to R.A.R. for design and development due to the many successes he had already achieved. Amongst these was a positively operated internal cam gear for valve operation, but this was not pursued due to its inherent mechanical objections. Another interesting engine was the Wankel engine, an eccentrically driven rotary conception. This project also was not pursued as I believe Mr. Railton although being interested in its rotary possibilities felt that the tooling necessary to produce the unusual case shapes, together with the probable difficulties involved in producing effective tip and end of rotor sealing precluded a firm of the comparatively small resources of T & T's from assisting in its development.

There was however the automatic gearbox presented by a Russian engineer, a certain Mr. Kamper, which was developed. This was a twin clutch, swinging layshaft, four-speed gearbox with vacuum servo control from the engine.

I well remember Mr. Kamper's frequent visits to the drawing office during this time when due to his unusual pronunciation of English his usual opening remark was "Any snakes" meaning any snags and there were plenty of these but it was initially fitted to a Morris 12 and made to work successfully. Due to its complication it was not taken

Fig. 16A *Bluebird secures world record.*

up by the Nuffield Organisation, but was to be later adopted by the Crossley Co. for truck use.

In 1937 J. B. Perrett left the firm to pursue the development of the "Robot" gearbox with Mr. Kamper. Sampietro could often be seen walking around the aerodrome deep in thought with problems possibly associated with solving by calculus methods the terminal speed of a vehicle, taking into account dozens of variables. He was to leave also and after designing a box frame with independent front suspension for the Healey car, he was eventually to go to America to settle down. They were both colleagues who were easy to get along with and I was sorry to see them go.

1934 saw the old tyre store by the "Chapel" occupied by Wally Hassan at work on "Babe" Barnato's Bentleys with the assistance of Jack Sopp, "borrowed" from T & T's. In stepping up the Bentley engine capacity from $6\frac{1}{2}$ to 8-litres he was soon becoming a threat to the success of John Cobb's Napier-Railton and perhaps temporarily to slow up this development I suggested to him, "Why not supercharge it?" A forward-facing air intake was fitted and later Wally commented to me in a slightly humorous but aggrieved tone, "You did not mention the pressure balancing of the float chambers!"

In the early 1930s another marque to receive attention both in the direction of design and tuning in the works was the MG Midget and Magnette. My first introduction to the Abingdon Design Personnel was one sunny morning when R.A.R. transported me in a well remembered straight eight open tourer Hudson of somewhat vivid red and orange hue (later to be agreed at the best colour for all round good visibility for other road users) and also at somewhat vivid speed, with my seat placed well back out of his elbow reach. It is conceivably possible that this was the first car in which R.A.R. eventually became involved with Noel Macklin and his aide Mr. Cushman in later producing the Railton car from basic Hudson engine unit and other items. It certainly gave me a good idea of Mr. Railton's ability as a safe but high speed driver, over the comparatively country roads from Brooklands to Abingdon. It also made me realise later what a wide variety of interests he had within the car industry, and also how huge was his capacity for specialist work. It was not the policy of the MG Co. however to engage directly in racing as was indicated by the then MG Chief, Mr. Kimber, in a paper he gave to the Institution of Automobile Engineers entitled

"Making Modest Production Pay in Motor Car Manufacture". He did however allow the "Magic Midget" to be produced—I believe at Cowley—to the body design of Mr. Railton, under "Jaray" patents, and this car with many different capacity engines was extremely successful, particularly in record runs when driven by Col. "Goldie" Gardner. I was involved in work on this car at a much later date as will be shown later. In the meantime people such as The Earl of March, Staniland, Horton, Bartlett, Hall Hamilton and many others were extracting better and better performances from these small cars with co-operation between themselves, the MG Company and T & T's.

The Land Speed Record car work was not to be left in abeyance as only a month after Sir Malcolm had taken the record at 301 m.p.h. R.A.R. was busy with calculations for a four-wheel drive car to be designed and built exclusively for this record for John Cobb. Five scale models were made to establish the minimum projected frontal area coupled with the surface area that could enclose the two supercharged Napier aero engines envisaged to power the car. They were known as A. "Three wheeler", B. "Cigar", C. "BB with troughs", D. "Long tail" and E. "Bun". The "Bun" was chosen after tunnel tests in the National Physical Laboratory, in spite of its somewhat larger projected area, but smaller surface area than some of the other models, and a $\frac{1}{8}$-scale layout was begun of the necessary machinery. To reduce the overall width of the car an ingenious method was devised by R.A.R. in that each engine was slung on either side of the central main frame, with each engine at 10° to the centre line of the car but staggered fore and aft in plan. This entailed an "S"-shaped frame in plan which was efficiently coped with in practice by the John Thompson Co. from the four sections, hot riveted together as per drawings supplied.

Before long I was joined by a Mr. Hobbs who took over the drawings required for the body. To maintain secrecy we now had a

Fig. 17 Overleaf *Photograph 17 shows Mr. John Cobb and Ken Taylor in discussion during the early days of the building of the car.*

Fig. 18 Overleaf *Photograph 18 is a front view of the car towards the end of its construction. This shows the independently sprung front wheels with their diagonal tie rods controlled by coil springs and rubbers. One propellor shaft rubber coupling and brake drum can be seen just to the left of the driving seat.*

Fig. 19 *Photograph 19 is a rear view of the car towards the end of its construction. The vertical cylinders just inboard of the rear wheels were to be used to operate an air brake. In practice the air brake was not used, as the motoring torque of the engines, together with the water cooled drum brakes were found to have ample capacity for the retardation required.*

lock on   the office door, using a hatch and a telephone for communication.

This hand-built body was a splendid piece of work, made by Bill Masters and one assistant only and with the assistance of ply formers made from drawings by Hobbs and resulted in a wonderfully smooth and accurate outline. It is conceivable that the seasoned and treated plywood was Vosper supplied as a result of work on Sir Malcolm Campbell's boat — but more of that later.

With the car now built the run-up test was dramatically stopped after a few seconds when P.T. noticed that no oil pressure was showing. R.A.R. immediately just said one word "alcohol!" and when the long capillary tube to the gauge was suitably primed the test proceeded satisfactorily.

I was informed soon afterwards that I was to be given the opportunity of going with Mr. Taylor and the car to America, as a

Fig. 20 *Photograph 20 shows Mr. John Cobb in the driving seat with R.A.R. in his usual thoughtful mood alongside. The Chassis, with the Body in the background, are both now nearing completion.*

holiday and to assist wherever possible. This was a terrific boost for me, and resulted in three of the most interesting months I can remember. The car was loaded on to the deck of the *Europa* out of Bremen, where it was possible to keep an eye on it, at Southampton. The four and a half days to New York went like a flash in company of P.T.'s friends "Taso" Mathieson, his brother, and a Mr. Snow, especially as we were allowed down in the engine room, at the captain's table and on the bridge, as well as a memorable star-room evening of champagne cocktails on the top-most deck.

Jimmy Rand and Bob Reading saw the car safely overland by rail whilst Mr. Taylor and I flew via United Air Lines to Salt Lake City, with an interesting night flight out of Chicago through an electrical storm. I was never quite sure whether the other sole occupant of the 32-seater plane—the stewardess—came over to reassure herself or ourselves, but the blue lightning flashes along the leading edge of the wing were a new experience for me, and remined me of crocuses. The vertical positive and negative accelerations were much less

Fig. 21 *The car being, or beginning to be unloaded at the Wendover Rail siding, Utah Salt Flats in a temperature of 110 degrees F. and at an altitude of about 4,000 feet.*

interesting. However we arrived safely at Salt Lake City the following day in sunshine to be transported to Wendover in a Hudson six, which company were to provide this car and a Hudson eight with Cotal box as transport for us as a result of Mr. Railton's liaison with that company in using some Hudson basic chassis items for the Railton car then being produced for sale to the general public.

We were soon installed in the Wendover garage on the south side of the road with sleeping accommodation in separate holiday cabins. The Dodge truck driven by Eddie Madsen, an easy-going American was used not only for transportation of material and men to the Salt Flats but also to provide a gangplank at the rear of it so that John Cobb could step down into the driver's seat of the Napier-Railton. The truck was also fitted with a tube and bar prong, swivelling but attached to the front fender, for push-starting the LSR car, and a towing eye at the rear for towing the car to and from the Flats.

Several trial runs were made, the first with much black smoke, necessitating altitude control, jet and plug changes by the Napier representative Joe Coe with Bob lending assistance, remarks being made about the accessibility of the inboard banks of cylinders. To assist gear changing the throttles were also set to give approximately 1,000 r.p.m. running light in neutral. Some trouble was also experienced with the cork floats being affected by the fuel used but it was not long before a high-speed run of some 250 m.p.h. was made. This resulted in noticeable air flow pressure dents in both the top and underside of the tail of the car. I was rather disappointed to see this, but R.A.R. seemed quite unperturbed saying that this showed that the attitude of the line of maximum body width to the ground must have been absolutely right as otherwise the denting would not have been so equally disposed. P.T. and I then extemporised with internal wooden fillers located with external but flush-fitting screws.

It was whilst this preparatory work was going on that the garage on the north side of the road became occupied by George Eyston and his crew headed by Bert Denly. The small town of Wendover was now becoming quite crowded with visitors and timing officials and Press, and it was at about this time that the Sheriff, a six feet four man called "high pockets", had his Indian motorcycle stolen. He was — to us — a friendly soul, so I thought this a good time to ask for the loan of his Colt .45, and during a lull in the work one early evening, Bob and I took it with a band of shells, into the mountains for practice.

The trick seems to be to sling it—not aim it—or to use both hands, but at least no damage was done, in my case not even to a tin-can, except that one or two rocks were spattered with lead.

It was also whilst Captain Eyston was making a run that I heard a woman visitor say to a friend when they were both looking at the front of the Napier-Railton. "Let's go round the back and look at the front!" The garage being open ended and shielded from visitors' entry by wire screens. These were light-hearted asides in pretty busy times, but at last we were ready for a timed run. To our dismay a very fast run was declared void as the car being of a similar shade to the back-ground salt it had not been registered on the timing gear and the timing officials insisted that the car have a black band painted along its sides. This was done and in addition an asbestos-backed, sheet-steel-faced plate was added to the tail to protect the light alloy body tail from the central exhaust flames. These modifications usually entailed trips into Salt Lake City for parts, but the Hudson cars performed wonderfully well in making the 130-mile journey in about two hours. Jimmy Rand once ran out of fuel and was offered a push by another car into Wendover by two—later to be discovered—merry men, which he reached in much faster time than he had intended even with surreptitious brake applications of the car he was driving.

Captain Eyston, who already held the record which he had taken in 1937 at 312 m.p.h., was now ready to go again and we were all rather taken aback when his two-way timed run was announced as 345.50 m.p.h. I knew that Mr. Railton considered that 350 m.p.h. was the terminal speed of the Napier, and this left a pretty small margin for taking the record from Eyston.

On September 15th, after a 3 a.m. call to allow plenty of time to get everything ready for a timed run (before the sun reached its 110° in the shade), the south to north run was completed successfully. The turn around was also within time and I hurried off in the Hudson at maximum speed about 100 yards west of the course line. I had almost reached the end of the mile timed section when with a woosh the Napier-Railton sped past, with a really shaking bow wave of air rocking the Hudson. Everyone was jubilant when the speed resulting from these two runs was given as 350.20 m.p.h.

Fig. 22 Opposite *The Napier-Railton outside its Wendover Garage.*

This completely vindicated Mr. Railton's work and prediction, John Cobb's driving and all the team's work. So everyone was happy for a while, but it was not long before it was known that Captain Eyston's crew were fitting their spare engine. I suggested to one of his team that the only way now for them was to seal up the front air entry—hoping that this would blow up the remaining engine. This was exactly what they were doing and R.A.R. and I called at their garage when the work was in progress. I was very amused when he asked if they would like a set of blueprints which he could supply! Unhappily this ruse was successful as the record was taken back again when Captain Eyston recorded, a two-way run for the mile of 357.50 m.p.h. I'm not quite sure who had the last laugh but I know that everyone who saw the Captain emerge from the cockpit at the end of this run could not have resisted a spontaneous laugh which his appearance gave of a "black and white minstrel" effect with his white overalled back but soot coloured face and front from the dust from his disc brakes being sucked through his driving compartment.

R.A.R. had further notions for increasing the speed of the Napier-Railton but John Cobb could not spend more time away from his fur broking business so it was decided to give up any further attempt for that year. A very good evening celebration given to both teams, shared and chaired by both John Cobb and Captain Eyston, showed that the local Americans appreciated the friendly rivalry that existed between the two teams in much the same way that we appreciated their friendly co-operation and hospitality. We had also had wonderful help from the Dunlop crew as usual headed by Mr. Fletcher, Dunlop "Mac" and "Sid" as well as the Shell representatives Ralph and Dave who also gave unstinted help with local supplies of ice for the project in addition to the help from local cafe and garage personnel. I'm not sure that the garage assistant appreciated us pointing out that the main garage building had a large notice stating "Rest Room"! The Press were also helpful, their photographers handing out many photographs gratis.

Now commenced the clearing up and here I was again to be given another boost when given the choice of either a trip to the Californian coast or a visit to the canyon country with Mr. Railton

Fig. 23 Opposite *Preparing for one of the early trial-runs. In this case more than the suggested number of eight persons assisting to mate the Body to the Chassis! The Dodge truck with the starter prong is alongside.*

and his wife with a friend Mrs. Clayton. P.T. had chosen to remain with the car and crew and we arranged to meet in New York before sailing home. After some delay in getting the right set of ignition keys we set off and met R.A.R. about 50 miles away lunching by the wayside. Yellowstone Park was interesting with its geysers and after seeing our third brown bear I said, "I suppose we've seen them all now," but it was not to be as upon stopping at a comfort station I was followed, but into the adjoining compartment (presumably by a female bear). This same bear later clambered on to the roof of the building in search of her cub, which she promptly knocked off with a swipe to the ground. I beat a fairly rapid retreat—R.A.R. saying that he "would not like a pat like that." The Colorado gorge has to be seen to be believed with its 14-mile-wide eroded valley up to a mile deep in places. The rock colouring and formation of canyons such as Zion are also truly remarkable. After several days R.A.R. was due for a pre-arranged trip to California and I was to leave his party to go by bus to Las Vegas. The young choir who sang me away from the hotel that we were departing from must have wondered why I did not respond as cheerfully to their departing cheer but did not realise, as I did at that moment, that Mr. Taylor had my return ticket from Salt Lake to New York, so I was thrown on my own resources more than 2,000 miles from our meeting point. However the bus duly deposited me at Las Vegas for a flight to Salt Lake City and the airport people could not have been more helpful in that they traced Ken Taylor by radio and even re-routed my flight via Detroit, where I was to visit the Hudson factory before flying on to New York via the Niagara Falls. Jimmy and Bob were met at the Times Square Hotel and due to the uncertain conditions of the European political scene Mr. Taylor became busy for a while in re-routing our return to England via the *Olympic*—a 10,000 ton British ship instead of the German *Bremen*. After another good crossing with only one rough day we were met and transported back to Brooklands by Jock Pullen through what now seemed to us to be narrow twisting country lanes, but welcoming all the same, as a conclusion of a truly memorable trip.

John Cobb was determined not to let the matter rest there and we were soon working on details to improve the performance of his LSR car. The chief of these was a replacement of the gearing driving the

Fig. 24 Opposite *R. A. Railton and J. R. Cobb inform the Press.*

supercharger impellors of the Napier engines and this work of increasing the blower speed was undertaken by the Napier Co. Practical experiments were undertaken in the shops to check the effect of the increased loading on the suspension and detail modifications made to the packing pieces under the composite coil springs and rubber discs, that were included in the original design, to balance the over-turning torque on the axle and so equalise the positive and negative accelerations during driving and braking with the resulting effect of more equal wear on the tyres. The top links on the rear suspension were also fitted with a limited spring controlled movement to avoid fight between the propeller shaft coupling and the five points, apart from the springs, by which the rear axle was suspended, and so reduce the possibility of synchronous vibration.

Mr. Taylor and crew duly left for America and on August 23rd, 1939, the modifications made were justified when the record was raised to 369.70 m.p.h.

Spec. of the Railton LSR Car (1938) and Material Suppliers.

Designer: R. A. Railton, Bsc, MIAE, MSAE. Builders: Thomson & Taylor (Brooklands) Ltd. Engines: Two Napier 12-cylinder $5\frac{1}{2}'' \times 5\frac{1}{8}''$ (23,936 c.c.), 1,250 h.p. Gearbox: Three speeds, top gear ratio, 1.35 to 1. Final drive: Back axle: bevel; shaft to front axle (four wheel drive). Tyres: 44″ Dunlop. Suspension: Independent at front, normal at rear. Fuel capacity: 18 gallons. Oil tank: 15 gallons. Water tank: 75 gallons. Wheelbase: 13′6″. Track: Front, 5′6″; rear, 3′6″. Overall length: 28′8″. Overall width: 8′. Overall height: 4′3″. Weight: 7,000lb. (dry). Body: 4 cwt. Total: Approx. $62\frac{1}{2}$ cwt. Weight/h.p.: Approx. 2.8lb. Air brake gear: Sir G. Godfrey & Partners Ltd. Ball and roller bearings: Hoffman Mfg. Co. Body material: Norther Aluminium Co. Ltd. (18 s.w.g. aluminium). Brake and shock-absorber linings: Ferodo. Brake-operating gear: Lockheed. Cockpit window: Triplex. Chassis frame: John Thompson Pressings Ltd. Fuel: National Benzole. High-tensile steel: Firth Derihon Stamping Ltd. Instruments, thermostats and fuel pipes: S. Smith & Sons Ltd. Magnetos: Lucas. Oil: Shell-B.P. Oil-seals: Super Oil Seal Mfg. Co. Ltd. Plugs: KLG. Special Controls and wheel-nuts: Simmonds Aerocessories Ltd. Steel tubes and light-alloy extrusions: Reynolds. Steering-gear: Burman. Steering gear links: Automotive Products. Springs: Tempered Steel Co. Ltd. Gears: David Brown. Universal joints: Laycock.

Much earlier in the year I had been introduced by Mr. Railton to an individual from a private firm who was keen to get his special transmission fitted to a cross-country track-laying vehicle and this unhappily in a way was to lead to six years of good war-time co-operation between T & T's and Her Majesty's Fighting Vehicles Design Establishment, amongst other branches of H.M. Forces.

Sadly it was now that I was to say goodbye to Mr. Railton who was to go to America with his wife and young family — Tim and Sally — to stay in California. Fortunately, our contact was to be maintained throughout the war years, to the advantage of the Allied war effort, and also in the following years of peace to my own gratification.

CHAPTER THREE

The War Years
1939-1945

The later part of 1938 was spent in detailing the transmission gear mentioned earlier, for a track laying and steering vehicle which was eventually to be installed in a War Office vehicle. At this time I was commuting between Brentford and Brooklands and the months rolled speedily by. The September 1939 War Declaration was etched on my memory, as on a Sunday morning, whilst journeying to Potters Bar to collect a repaired Haynes five valve receiver, the air raid alarm sirens blasted off, but this was apparently a false alarm as no raiders were seen. However, it meant that my small car runs were to be restricted in future, due to fuel rationing and I was soon installed in lodgings in Byfleet adjacent to the Track.

Almost immediately the very damaging air raid on the Vickers Works on the other side of the Track took place one morning in daylight, when the eight raiders swept in low down from the East and away to the West, clearly visible across the 'drome, without opposition of any kind; followed by the echo of the bombs from the Aerodrome Hanger Buildings by the Thomson & Taylor Workshops and the dust cloud from the devastation. This was a sad jolt to our efforts, but I believe served to renew them, particularly as it was ironically suggested that the German pilots concerned in the raid were trained at the Brooklands School of Flying run by Mr. Henderson before the War. Shortly afterwards a few Air Force dirigibles were installed around the Track and later camouflage work was commenced to disguise the concrete circuit from the air — a fairly long term project.

In order to speed up the experimental tank transmission project we were now to be assisted by two senior members of the Staff of the Fighting Vehicle Design Establishment and were joined by Mr. G. V. Cleare and Mr. Bentley. For this work we were moved back into the old "Parry Thomas" Drawing Office and before long the transmission was ready for installation in a vehicle. I remember feeling elated that we were to be loaned a vehicle shell complete with engine and tracks in order that T & T could complete the work of producing a running vehicle, but was soon deflated when the Brooklands Authorities questioned the possible damage to the Track when the vehicle, weighing a good many tons would have to be moved around it to get to the Workshops. This objection was, however, soon waived aside with Dr. Merritt's help when it was pointed out that the unit loading on the Track was of no more a serious order than the loading of a human foot, when the work of getting the prototype vehicle into the Shops was carried on. This was accomplished by entering via the Sewage Works Entrance by the Byfleet Station, over a very small culvert — with anxiety — and through a double door entrance in the Railway Straight, which was hardly wide enough for the Transporter, but with great expertise the Truck support Army driver literally inched the ten inch square oak gatepost upright again after the Transporter had entered and we were soon established in the Workshops.

This was the first of five experimental Tank transmissions that T & T's were to build over the following years and included the first Tank of one type to accomplish 1,000 miles of Test running without breakdown, chiefly due to good co-operation with H.M.F.V.D.E. headed by Dr. Merritt and by very good work in the T & T machine shop and fitting shop headed by Mr. Ken Taylor with mechanics Ted Bradbury and his assistant Peter Horne. During this period a road had been cut through the Brooklands Track just to the West of the Byfleet foot bridge, to provide a second entrance to the Vickers hangars now also built on the Track. This new roadway, incidentally, provided an easier entrance for heavy vehicles into the T & T Workshops, although a Pickford Transporter on H.M. Service did manage to get grounded on a grassy hump when bringing the new experimental hull of a non-runner into the Works at about 2 o'clock one wet morning. These Army R.E.M.E. non-commissioned Staff were always a joy to meet for their determination to get the job done and for their bonhomie in doing it. I remember one sergeant who, although having lost some stripes, which apparently was caused through ignoring the park like condition of the Colonel's lawn with a tank, was still just as efficient as ever at completing his task without them as he was with them before.

In addition to the dirigibles, machine gun emplacements were added at strategic points near the hangars. T & T themselves provided a make-shift air raid shelter by placing timbers across a boundary sewage ditch, covered with corrugated iron and turf, which, with its well sighted, open ended construction could provide some shelter from the total of seven raids, later to be made across the Track. It was once a source of bizarre amusement to see the machine gun tracer bullets reaching about fifty feet into the air with a German bomber circling unconcernedly above them. Later still a low flying bomber aircraft could be seen weaving in and out of the balloons and finally drop a sizeable bomb directly on to the Track. This made a skating contact with the concrete, then bounced directly into and through the brick built end wall of a Vickers hangar recently built — fortunately without exploding. This may conceivably have inspired Dr. Barnes Wallis to develop the bouncing bomb that did so much damage later on to the German water system.

After the first Tank transmission had been detailed, produced, fitted and run in its experimental form, T & T's were kept in touch with the F.V.D.E. but their two assistant Design Members were withdrawn, when I returned to the previously occupied Office in the "Hermitage" building. Shortly afterwards a morning raid took place at almost exactly nine o'clock. I was about to set out from my digs when the sound of alarm and bombs occurred almost simultaneously. It was obvious that the bombs had exploded very close to the T & T Workshop, so as the noise died away I hurried over to see what damage had been done. The first sign was a large crater where a building leased by R. G. J. Nash with a sign entitled "The Horseless Carriage Corporation" had once been. No loss of life here, as nobody was in the building at the time, but on moving on I noticed that my office roof, about fifty yards away was enfolding a very early Mercedes motor car, possibly of 19th century vintage, in its tarred felt, wood and asbestos structure. Nobody in the T & T Works was hurt either — they started work at 8.30 a.m. and were all about to take shelter when the raid occurred, but Jimmy Rands was lucky as Mr. Taylor had just given him his steel helmet — one of the few available — when it was knocked firmly on to his head by a piece of flying debris. R. G. J. Nash later remarked to me, "It was the most unwarlike building on the whole of the Track." This slightly aggrieved remark seemed to sum up the whole of this particular raid.

The Teds Bradbury and Underwood soon had the office clear, when I moved across the corridor into what had been Mr. Railton's office with the damaged part of the roof temporarily covered with a tarpaulin. The remainder of the raids were across the aerodrome grass where this — as the aerodrome, was not officially operational — was the best place for them.

Here I should mention that Ted Bradbury's name is mentioned not only to show how keen was his outlook generally, but particularly on the Tank work, on which he was the Chief Mechanic with Peter Horne as his assistant. He was just as ready to help to get the office clear of debris as he was to tune the carburetters of a new type tank engine. It was really due to their able and enthusiastic fitting work in the Shops that any success was achieved.

During the early years of the War I was still able to spend an occasional weekend at the home of my parents at Brentford as this could match a necessary visit to Pattern Makers and Founders in the near vicinity, to assist in the progress of the various jobs. On a couple of these visits we were disturbed by air raids. The first being by a raid by incendiary bombs, which I believe were really targeted on the closely adjoining railway line, but they created some moderate excitement, as at the time there was information that explosive incendiaries were being used. This was not, however, the case with this raid, but I was somewhat dismayed when dumping sand on bombs in the rear garden to be informed, "Mr. Beauchamp your roof is on fire!" Sure enough the front of the roof was holed and its beams smoking from one of the bombs. A neighbour's hand pump was soon dealing with this but it was not long before the A.R.P. men were on the scene and the resulting ceiling glow extinguished. As the neighbour's name was Marshall, it became clear, much later, that this was an early example of generous Marshall aid which was gratefully accepted. The second raid, however, was not so easily dealt with as a high explosive bomb was dropped about forty yards away, with doors and windows being blown in from the air blast and with glass and plaster everywhere. This made the house quite uninhabitable, so the following weekend my brother and I moved everything across to his home at Isleworth, about two miles away. Shortly afterwards whilst making another visit to the old house to make it reasonably secure I was making my way back to Isleworth on foot, when a string of bombs was dropped along the main Isleworth

Road and I imagined my brother's house had been hit. This, however, was not the case, but in hurring back along the main road, an enormous pillar of flame from a broken gas main at the entrance to the Duke of Northumberlands' Parkland Estate was the unfortunate funeral pyre of an unknown pedestrian.

This was the total nastiness suffered from enemy bombardment from the air, although during the later years it was strangely encouraging, but odd, to have to trust to luck, when on foot during a raid, that one might escape from the hail of shrapnel from our own anti-aircraft guns. Much later on we were fortunate, when moving around, to escape the "Doodle Bug" nonsense both in London and in Surrey.

Reverting to the work on tanks, this was continued in 1941 with experimental transmission work on a Canadian Type Churchill Tank. This was an unfortunate project as far as personal injuries were concerned as Peter Horne, who was assisting in the Works, had lost the top of a finger through the driver entrance cover falling on it and later I was unfortunate enough to fall on to the rough cut side of it, being bounced to the ground after being partially stopped by its side wall edge and an old compound fractured shin. The resulting marrow infection kept me away for three months. Fortunately the work was almost complete, so I was able to spend the time doing light jobs, such as wiring up an Anderson shelter for lighting and heating in my brother's garden, as my parents had said that, "I am not going to sit in a damp hole in the ground for anyone, certainly not for Hitler!" Events later proved that the shelter did not have to be used.

Upon my return, Mr. Ken Thomson, who had just established a new residence at East Horsley in Surrey, suggested that I stay with him, his brother Roy, David Courage and Mr. Freeman—a locally based solicitor, to which I was pleased to agree. We were to make up a very amicable quintet of people, with visits from Mr. Ken Taylor and T & T associated visitors at various times, all busily engaged in pursuing the war effort. Among the visitors was Mr. Henry Spurrier, Managing Director of the Leyland Co., who was also responsible for giving me a hairy ride on the offside front "wing" of a Cromwell Tank prototype, that had just been completed at the T & T Workshops. This took place at the Brooklands Aerodrome, when I was pretty taken aback at the speed at which we motored around, as no running in had taken place before hand, but all was well and he seemed delighted with the model.

Leisure time included amateur work in the garden to assist a part time gardener with fruit and vegetable care, to support the establishment with its housekeeper and help. Another activity was to build up an old bee-hive, and with the help of a local bee keeper to keep a hive of bees to aid the fertilisation of fruit in the garden. This hive was later increased to three, but probably because of lack of time to attend to them all properly they were eventually invaded by a swarm of wild bees from the adjoining woods. Because of either an invading queen bee, or local vandalising interference, the resulting disturbance of the hives was such that in an effort to see what the trouble was, I was attacked in no small way and given a beard of stings, which with a final queenly jab in the ear knocked me out for the second time in my life. The eighteen pounds of honey we totally secured hardly seemed to be worth the trouble, but the fruit trees seemed to flourish.

After 1942-3 the tank prototype work tailed off, and here it seems very appropriate to mention in connection with tank design work generally, but particularly with regard to the Churchill Tank, what enormously good work Dr. Merritt had been responsible for whilst heading the F.V.D.E. It was particularly encouraging, on the few occasions on which I was to meet him, how gracious and efficient he was in dealing with private industry staff such as myself. The same was true, when visiting David Brown & Co. at Huddersfield, of Dr. Tuplin, and appropriately enough the Chief of the Design Staff at the Albion Company.

Overlapping the tank work was another interest, in that T & T's were to build a storage hangar to house the flow of Hall Scott Marine Engines that were coming in from America as a result of Mr. Railton's liaison with that company and the Admiralty. This was also combined with Mr. Noel Macklin's work (who had co-operated with Mr. Railton in peace-time on building the Railton car) to build sectionalised M.T.B. wooden hulls to be powered by the Hall Scott Engines, at a near-by factory. From now on our main task was to recondition, cannibalise and re-build these Hall Scott Engines, with some additional experimental work involving the supercharged version. This involved a small scheme of change to combat the throttles freezing up on these models, but they were later phased out, to improve the boats' reliability and range. At about this time news was filtering through of the heroic exploits of Lt. Commander

Hutchens and his kind, who were doing valiant work in combating the U-Boat menace with these boats.

The "Chapel" building alongside the main Workshop had been adapted to accommodate a test bench to check test all engines after build, as a crowning effort of Bob Readings and his team after all their good fitting work. This was followed by very helpful liaison with Thames Side Boat Builders who were installing the engines. As a result of this work I was fortunate enough to be included with Mr. Taylor in a trip to Weymouth to witness a practical run out to sea with an operational M.T.B. that had been generously arranged by a naval representative. With a fine day and a choppy sea, the flat out run to test the water circulation was a great success, with no interference from enemy action. The admirable handling of the Boat, by a very young Lt. Commander left me with a great deal of admiration, and envy.

Another scheme for the improved reliability of under water weapons initiated by Mr. Railton was produced and tested and showed promise that further development could be of value. This project was later pursued by Commander Gray of the Naval Authorities. It is also possible that this work could have been tied in with the good work that the T & T machine shops did in machining a number of steel forgings of complicated shape that were used in the landing gear of the Swordfish aircraft, as a result of Mr. Taylor's liaison with the Design Staff of the Fairey Aviation Co. which resulted in successful attacks on the German Naval shipping.

At this time we were allowed a slim ration of petrol, that allowed us to move around a little more freely and this was very useful, as a new depot had been started up at Sutton, with the assistance of the Ministry of Supply, when occasional visits were made to get the depot established, under the guidance of Mr. Taylor. This depot was engaged solely in the supply of naval requirements.

The Cobham Depot of T & T's was also expanded by adding a small machine shop with, amongst others, a new "Do-All" continuous band saw machine, that added to the speed of supply of certain items. The Roycott Seed & Fruit Protection Co. at nearby Downside was also opted into supplying guards for these potentially dangerous machines, when operated by feminine labour.

A further large building was also erected at Brooklands to house three test benches for the Hall Scott Engines, with good assistance

from the Heenan & Froude Co. A travelling crane was also arranged
to transport the finished assembled engines the hundred yards or so
from the fitting shop in the Chapel to the new building. It was soon
discovered by Bob Readings that the best way to transport this
weighty piece of mechanism with its three ton engine assembly was to
enlist the old shop runabout, an ancient 12 h.p. Austin Saloon car.
This adaptation was quite effective and certainly cheaper in cost and
time than producing a self propelled crane. Such was the lively co-
operation throughout the Works.

A corner of this new building was used to house a carbon arc flame
cutter which was arranged with some very good help from a local
electrician, Mr. Causey, who lent his knowledge of the mains supply,
and installed the control gear for this project. It was used to cut up
and so salvage the light alloy metals from enemy aero-engines, which
were now being shot down and collected from all over the country. It
was an encouraging sight to notice as the war progressed, how day by
day, this pile of scrapped engines increased in size. This feeling of
elation was offset by the sight of a number of Wellington bombers,
now being built at the Vickers Works, being returned by the R.A.F.
after being crashed or shot down and now operated on by T & T
Works people who were also salvaging the light alloy parts, in what
had been the T & T Running Shed at the Track. Jock Pullen was in
charge of this work and was responsible for a fabric curtain being
arranged so that visitors to this Shop who were in danger from flying
rivets being hammered out of the geodetic sections, could have some
sort of protection. The sadness at the sight of these aircraft, some in
terribly mangled and blood stained condition, was again offset when
it became known that larger and larger bombs were being
successfully dropped on enemy territory as a result of bomb gear
which was produced mainly in the T & T Workshop, close by the
Running Shed, as a result of close collaboration with the Vickers Co.
by Ken Taylor. Work on parachute harness may also, perhaps, have
assisted in helping to save the lives of some of these aircraft crews.

During most of this time we had been a Design Drawing and
Progress Office of two, with Peter Horne as an apprentice, but
during the 1944 period the naval work was progressed by a friend of
Mr. Thomson in the person of Mr. G. Kenway and this allowed me to
return to tank transmission design work with Mr. Clerk of the
Hydraulic Coupling and Engineering Co. of Isleworth under the

technical and business guidance of Mr. Sinclair, a director of the company. Their Self Synchro Shift mechanism was not only incorporated in tank and "Duck" amphibious vehicles but also in two speed and reverse gear (for speed control) marine gearboxes. These were interesting projects in which to be involved in their experimental stage.

Another minor task was to extract as much power as possible (without major modification) from a small Hillman four cylinder engine to allow it to be built into a crawler vehicle which was to carry a remote controlled high explosive charge to be directed against the enemy emplacements.

At about this time, it was marvellous occasionally to meet members of H.M. Armed Forces at the White Lion Hotel at Cobham, close by the T & T Station, as well as Ministry of Supply people, who were entertained to lunch by Mr. Ken Thomson, whose office was located at Cobham. K.J.T. must have had many headaches in managing the financial affairs of the company as the number of works personnel was now increased to more than 100 as compared to about thirty in the days of Parry Thomas. It is conceivable that he too received a lift from the confident attitude of H.M. Forces men as well as from the guarded, but helpful attitude of the Ministry Staff.

From the work that we were now getting it was becoming obvious that the allied war effort was now reaching a successful climax. I was soon to be offered a trip with the invasion forces, by an American representative of the Hall Scott Co., but regretfully refused — being concerned that a civilian might be a drag on the organisation. As a matter of history, the surrender of Germany eventually followed, when on 8th May, 1945 I was informed by telephone from Cobham that the war was over. Most of the staff foregathered at Cobham for a celebratory drink, when the whole of the works were given the rest of the afternoon off. I spent a relaxed hour or two in a deck chair in the sunshine of "Cheriton" garden, feeling that at last the "spring" could become unwound.

CHAPTER FOUR

The Post War Years
1945-1949

The following few months were a strange period of let down, with the eventual shattering knowledge of what mankind was capable of, when the nuclear bombing of Japan resulted in their final surrender on the 15th August that same year.

We were now in the painfully slow period of clean-up and re-establishment of peace time days. The first depot to be phased out gradually was the naval one at Sutton, but this was to the advantage of the Brooklands Design Office as Norman Walker was to join the staff with Gowan Kenway, so with Peter Horne, we were now a useful team of four. The work for H.M. Naval Forces, however, continued at Brooklands as we were, under a Reparation Scheme, to be given the task of building, re-building or cannibalising the 'E' Boat engines handed over by the German Navy to the British forces. In addition to this fitting work in the Shops it became necessary to adapt the Test Benches in the new building, now known for some obscure reason as "The College" possibly because work for all three of H.M. Forces went on in this building. This adaptation not only allowed all engines to be tested after build but also enabled oil consumption tests to be carried out (after alterations had been effected on pistons and rings) in addition to the usual power curves and fuel oil consumption tests. The modifications made (including a de-rating of the engine power) resulted in an engine that was acceptable for some of H.M. Naval Forces requirements. Not only did we receive these engines but also a number of very fine machine tools, including a magnetic crack testing machine which we modified to re-orientate its performance. Unexpectedly we were also assisted in this work by a German technician, a very good and helpful engineer. It was interesting to reflect, how at the beginning of the war, my thoughts were that our navy was at a disadvantage to its German counterpart, in that they had more powerful steel hulled M.T.Bs., compared with our less powerful wooden hull craft; but after experience with these 'E' Boat engines, with their large bore, with twin banks of cylinders set at an unusual angle, in a necessarily long crank and case assembly, (which could and did result in some quite noticeable torsional vibration), it seemed to me that their construction was probably pushed ahead by uninformed authority, and this may have assisted our naval personnel in their valiant task, during the war.

War time contacts with the Leyland Co. were extended in these days when the Chief Engineer of that Company—Mr. Pilkington—assisted in progressing contact already established by Ken Thomson and Mr. H. Spurrier, with Ken Taylor and the T & T Design Department. This resulted in three different but similar projects being produced, all using the 7.4 litre 6 cylinder Leyland Diesel Engine as a power source. The first requirement was for a power unit and clutch assembly, which could be transported to drive pumps or such like machinery, wherever required. The photographs show its final assembly. The second was of a self-contained, transportable Generator Set for use anywhere in this country or abroad.

Fig. 25 *Near side of 7.4 litre 6 cylinder Leyland diesel engine and clutch—portable assembly with power take off for general purposes.*

Fig. 26 *Off side of same unit.*

Fig. 27 *Off side of similar Leyland engine adaptation for transportable generator set.*

Fig. 28 Overleaf *Adaptation of Leyland diesel engine for marine purposes with American twin-disc clutch, and forward and reverse gear.*

The photograph shows this complete arrangement. The third was a Marine Engine adaptation which used an American Twin Disc Clutch and Forward and Reverse Gearbox as a complete unit to form the assembly as shown.

Once again Mr. Railton was involved in this smooth co-operation with our American friends in the supply of the necessary American items. We were still economising in fuel — as rationing was still in force. The supply of materials, especially high quality steel, was also in very short supply and in addition the progressing of many items that could have been speeded up by a direct call was difficult to arrange.

Through a Thames-side boat builder, with whom we had co-operated during the war, we were able to test one of these marine units by installing it in an old open hull lifeboat, when the test on the Thames was concluded satisfactorily, without any modifications being required to be made. The long propellor shaft, however, with no centre bearing and made from large diameter gas piping, did not enhance its free running performance. I believe the Leyland Co. later used this model to start a Marine Section in their Special Projects Division.

It was quite extraordinary how frequently the experience of war time products had a bearing on peace time tasks, when through Mr. Taylor, and possibly through his continuing contacts with the R.A.F. Cadets, we were soon involved with the Hillman Co. in producing car controls for the Hillman Minx type of model, for use by ex-servicemen who had been unfortunate enough to have been disabled through the war. This work was mostly undertaken by Norman Walker. Here our war-time experience had shown us what good figures of manifold depression this engine gave, when a suitable Dewandre Vacuum Servo Motor provided power to operate the controls. The picture of the driving compartment, resulting from the painstaking work put in by Norman Walker as well as the close attention both he and Mr. Taylor gave to the best way to cope with the controls for the various permutations of loss of either one or more limbs by the potential driver, shows the totality of the controls that could be supplied to suit most disabled drivers requirements. 1. is a hand control that could be hooked up to either clutch or accelerator by movement in one or another plane. 2. is a hand control to operate the foot brake. 3. and 4. pedals could be arranged to operate either the clutch or the foot brake. 5. is a vacuum gauge and 6. 7. and 8.

are standard controls. This was a sad task in which to be involved, but it was marvellous to see how grateful almost all of these ex-servicemen were to be able to drive again after their rehabilitation.

Fig. 29 *Cars for various combinations of loss of limb or limbs by drivers. The text describes via numbers shown the function of each control.*

One Sunday afternoon in the early summer of 1946 I arrived back at Cheriton, T & T's war-time quarters, to find John Cobb in conversation with Ken Thomson. He almost immediately handed me a sketch—obviously from Mr. Railton—saying, "What do you think of that?" I could see that this was a simple objective scheme to keep the engines running during gear-changes for Q.5000—as the Land Speed Record car was known in the works—and just said, "marvellous." It then transpired that we were to go ahead with producing the scheme in conjunction with Mr. Railton's co-operation from America for another go at the LSR.

The following week the body and chassis were unearthed from a country barn where they had been stored during the war years, and a very woebegone sight it was from years of dust, but as the vital metal parts had been lacquered to prevent salt erosion the car had survived really well. The engines had been stored in T & T's workshops for about seven years and these, when opened up (as will be described later), were both in excellent condition due to careful attention in this interim period.

At this juncture it might be as well to explain, that, although the car had done all and more than was asked of it (it was originally designed for 350 m.p.h.), there was the possibility of a snag arising in this way. The engines were originally designed for aircraft use with propellers, but as there was no such flywheel effect in the car with each engine driving through a free wheel it was found very difficult with the gear in neutral during gear-changes to keep the engines running, before selecting the next gear. If the engines died during this stage there was no means of bringing them back to life. This did happen on one occasion in spite of an increase in the slow-running throttle position and proved to be expensive in both time and money as the run then had to be cancelled. The R.A.R. scheme would obviate this possibility and was arranged as follows. A twin vee-belt drive was to be taken from the propeller shaft on the output side of the gearbox, to drive a shaft over the gearbox which in turn, via a removable dog, was to drive the outer ring of a free wheel, through a 7:1 gear train, mounted on the engine output shaft. With this arrangement, should either engine speed fall below 1/7 of the propellor shaft speed, the momentum of the respective wheels that each engine had been driving would be utilised to pick up the engine concerned and maintain it at that speed whilst gear-changing, so that upon reopening the throttle after gear-changing both engines were certain to be alive.

A start was made on the engine end of the scheme, and the first problem to arise was the time honoured one of getting a quart into a pint pot, without using sawdust (a Jock Pullen riddle). This arose as, although the crankcase was suitable for an airscrew shaft gear, the output housing — due to it being a direct-drive engine — was not. It was obvious, however, that it was essential to retain the existing output-shaft housing in its entirety, due to the fact of there being no room between the engine and gearbox for additional gearing and also because this housing was a complicated item with its output shaft, bearings, oil-feed, breather, and magneto drives and supports.

A preliminary scheme was made, and this showed good prospects of the space available within the crankcase being sufficiently large for the purpose. Great encouragement was given here by Ken Taylor agreeing to make the necessary arrangements to hand-machine away certain parts of the crankcase to accommodate a housing for the gearing to be added and with this modification the required room was found for it. The crankshaft being fed by oil from both ends — it was possible to make good use of the front oil-feed that had been used to lubricate the not now used reduction gearing by stopping up these jets and leading a fresh oilway from the crankshaft end directly into the centre of the roller-type free wheel in order to ensure that this member was adequately lubricated, as the speed difference here between adjacent parts was a maximum. The high speed input shaft, with its manually "freeable" dog by an external control, and its intermediate shaft and gear were all housed in an alum-bronze housing combining oil galleries for their bearing lubrication. Special roller bearings and bronze cages were made for this application. The external control for the freeable dog was included to avoid the engines being rotated when the car was being towed to the Salt Flats. The co-operation of the Napier Co. was then asked for and very willingly given after a visit to the Acton works by Mr. John Cobb, Ken Taylor and myself, and it was very pleasant to re-meet Tony Hall of Napier's after so many years and to receive all the marvellous help that he and that company were able to give. This engine end of the scheme was approved by Mr. Railton in America with his usual pointed comments during its development and eventually all the details and the two engines were handed over to Napier's for complete manufacture. I recall one very bold decision made by them when the engines were completely dismantled and the master connecting rod main white-metal bearings were replaced as examined in spite of minute settling cracks which their experience prompted them to leave alone.

Whilst this work was going on at Napier's the scheme for the driving end was proceeded with. The August holiday now seemed to be a good time to have a few days rest, so with a Morris car loaned by Ken Thomson I visited David Courage in Dorset who had been one of five bachelors K.J.T. had been good enough to have made up a happy "menage" with at Cheriton, East Horsley, during the war. It later turned out to be a regrettable decision to take out a hired skiff for a sail in Weymouth Bay as the leaky old lug sail-boat proved no match for the wind and wave conditions of the Chesil race and with an inexperienced crew we managed to capsize it. More unfortunately, in my case, I managed to get entangled with the propeller of a rescuing launch, suffering rib and shoulder blade fractures, and waking up in hospital about five hours later. However, I could still walk and managed to return when expected back at Brooklands. The hernia that later developed was also somewhat restricting, especially when making efforts to find a supplier for the essentially narrow reinforced rubber vee-belts for the drive from the propeller-shaft pulley. These belts had to be of narrow width as a body bulkhead limited the space which they could occupy, apart from other reasons. Eventually R.A.R. and John Cobb were responsible for getting a dozen belts of the required size from America, manufactured by the Goodyear Co., and these were one of the few items not of British manufacture, but were gratefully welcomed.

The top pulley-bearing was supported off two canti-levered channel section members, which in turn were supported by two "A" brackets bolted to each side of each gearbox, with a cross-tube tie. The rear belt assembly also had a threaded adjustment for the belts with a cover over to shield the belts from any contact when the body was mated with the chassis. These two assemblies, i.e. the belt drive assembly and the engine unit gear assembly were coupled with a Hardy Spicer small-size propeller-type shaft to complete it. The whole arrangement for each engine weighed 100lb. — but as this was equally disposed about the existing centre of gravity of the car the added weight would be of advantage from an adhesion point of view as in 1938 I had seen that on accelerating away from a push start intermittent tyre rubber markings could be seen on the salt at explosion load intervals.

The works had during this time been busy dismantling and minutely examining the axles and gearboxes of the chassis. Hair line cracks were found in the front axle casing but as it was proposed to fit a different axle ratio the opportunity was taken to replace this light alloy casting with one of RR_{53} and also make room for the new bevel gears. The gearbox bearings all showed signs of wear which also showed how narrow was the safety margin in keeping weight to a minimum in the original design. The bearings were replaced and upgraded where necessary by filling the races with rollers and dispensing with cages. The gearbox output roller free-wheel back-up flaps were replaced by up-grading their material and fitting stronger return springs. The brake drums were skimmed and linings replaced. The body of the car was also given close attention, particularly regarding the riveting of the belt around the body through which the engines took their air. All these many rivets were either re-set or replaced which was again instituted by a comment from R.A.R. and was certainly justified when, after the record was taken, the body sides around the belt-area were seen to have a noticeable bulge! For the engine driving the front wheels to have better access to this air an aircraft type reinforced linen cover over one of the large lightening holes in this belt was removed, which leads one to the thought that adhesives must have been good even in those days.

Everything now being ready, it was decided to give the engine driving the rear wheels a run up to test the new anti-stalling gear. This took place on Sunday, 22nd June, 1947 but regrettably was to end in calamity when, perhaps because of the noise and smoke, the main drive free-wheel lock was let into engagement before the rear wheels had stopped. The resulting circulating torque parted the top bevel gears of the camshaft drive to the left hand cylinder block. This was the weakest link in the chain, and the most easily replaceable item, which R.A.R. had foreseen when the anti-stalling gears, buried in the heart of the engine, were designed. This was a sad setback, as a Press review had been arranged for the following week. It was decided to replace the cylinder head complete when the car reached America, and a short while later I was to spend a late Saturday evening locating Bob Reading and with his assistance getting the required cylinder head dismantled from the Brooklands spare engine for despatch to America. This disaster was hard to take as, upon being asked by John Cobb, I had optimistically said that I did not think (knowing how much good work Napier's had put into

Fig. 30 Opposite *The photograph shows the Napier-Railton at Brooklands just before being loaded on to a transporter to begin its journey to America. John Cobb with Ken Thomson and Ken Taylor on his left, is shown with all the Works crew who had been involved with the car build. The smiles on the faces of those nearest the camera were prompted by; ironically enough, a small dog running loose by the camera-man. John Cobb being his usual imperturbable self.*

building the engines) that it would be necessary to send the spare engine over to America. However, recalling the Kipling motto of the Wimbledon Tennis Club about treating triumph and disaster the same, I was encouraged by the fact of the project continuing and forwarded all relevant details on to R.A.R. in America. There were numerous items to which he would give his expert guidance, such as whether to retain the half a degree nose-up attitude of the body, attention to the Geecen tachograph recorder, how much ice to carry (the ice tank held 75 gallons, and had previously only been half-filled), the shock-absorber settings and many other items, including the retention or increase in size of the $\frac{1}{8}''$ hole in the sides of the driver's canopy through which the air exited (after entry through the base of the canopy) from the otherwise sealed driving compartment.

After the usual trial runs and adjustments on the Bonneville Salt Flats the record was taken at 394.20 m.p.h. on 16th September, 1947, in conditions of track that were far from perfect. The tachograph showed that for the first time a speed of over 400 m.p.h. had been reached by a land vehicle driven through its wheels by internal combustion engine means. This was a terrific effort of John Cobb's as not only did the tachograph show a maximum speed of 410-412 m.p.h. but it also showed that around that speed considerable vibration (probably of second or third order) had occurred in spite of the fact that the engine driving the front wheels took its drive through five flexible rubber couplings and the engine driving the rear wheels did so through three similar-type flexible couplings. At that speed the engines would have been turning at more that 4,000 r.p.m. and this from an engine whose basic crank-rod and piston assemblies had been originally designed for 1,800 r.p.m. When the car returned to this country I noticed that the steering drag-link — previously clearing the back of J.C.'s driving seat by about one inch had quite obviously been chafing the back of it due to the gyroscopic flick from the front wheels in spite of them being severely restricted in vertical movement. After the record was taken the congratulatory letter I had from Mr. Railton said, "Everything was perfect!"

This LSR of 1947 was the first of the records with which the author was concerned at the conclusion of World War II. The following year another interesting project was first broached by Ken Taylor when the plan to fit an up-to-2-litre unsupercharged Jaguar engine unit in Col. Gardner's MG "Magic Midget" original chassis was suggested.

This car is probably sufficiently well known not to need much description. It is an MG Magnette chassis with the transmission set at an angle in plan view to allow the driver to sit alongside the propeller shaft in an almost reclining attitude in order to keep the projected frontal area of the body to a minimum. The car with its really fine, smooth outline was designed by Mr. Railton, and before the record attempt here described, already held a great number of class records, when driven by its owner, Col. "Goldie" Gardner.

The Jaguar engine was larger in all respects than the engine it replaced and the first problem was how to dispose the increased height and depth within the existing body lines. It was decided to allow the standard oil-sump to protrude through the undershield by half an inch and make a new fairing over the camshaft covers, an inch above the existing line, and raise up the cockpit cover over the driver's head by a similar amount to maintain the same view as before of the road ahead. It would probably have been preferable to provide a new oil sump to be enclosed by the existing undershield as the records it was envisaged that the car would take would all be of short distances. But the Jaguar Co. was keen to ensure that the engine unit should be absolutely standard in all respects. The body and undershield were eventually suitably stiffened up with light alloy top-hat-section members where the necessary cut-outs required it.

Having decided on the line that the transmission should take in side view, and as the line in plan view was already laid down by the angle of the rear axle pinion relative to the centre line of the car, it only remained to settle the fore and aft position of the engine, to complete the rough general layout. It was found that if the engine and gearbox unit were placed as far forward as possible, the weight distribution on the front and rear wheels at speed would be substantially as before. This encouraging fact was achieved by substituting a rear engine supporting cross-member and another front engine cross-member, such that they offset the mass of the previously existing blower that had of necessity been placed forward of the front axle. As the road on which the car was to run in Belgium had bends at both ends of the course, the removal of the blower from its position ahead of the front axle was viewed with particular satisfaction.

Now that the position of the power unit in the frame was fixed, it was found very difficult to find space for frame cross-members between the front and rear of the unit, but room for a small cross-member was found ahead of the unit to improve the torsional rigidity of the frame, the side members of which could have been likened to the proverbial pepper-pot, due to the many combinations of engine that had been fitted to the car during its long (approx. 18 years) history of record performances.

Estimations of the various forces on the front and rear mountings were then made. It was decided not to use the existing rubber mounting but to allow all transverse forces to be taken through the rear engine mounting, and so through the frame where its sections were most suitable for taking care of them. To this end a bracket supporting a free-fitting ball was secured to the front of the engine casing. This ball was then made a sliding and rotatable fit on the top pin support of two pierced-steel members that formed a link, the lower pin of which was supported in a trunnion mounting below the centre of the front engine-mounting cross-member. Use was made of the trunnion mounting central rib in that it was cut away to act as a limiting stop for the link angular movement. The height of the ball mounting, and consequently the link length, was decided by a line in side view which passed through the front ball mounting, the node of the crankshaft, and the centre line of the rear engine trunnion. The rear engine unit mounting was made of a welded and machined-up steel member with a split cap, which in turn was located on the rear unit cross-member by split flanges suitably located. With this arrangement all torsional shocks emanating from the road wheels could only be transmitted through the frame and not through the crankcase.

Whilst work on these new parts was going on the axle ratio was changed and the chassis examined and prepared for the fitting of them. Additions and modifications to items such as petrol, oil and water systems, as well as controls were all progressed to match the delivery time of the power unit. With regard to the cooling system there was the fortuitous fact that the long and comparatively large diameter piping from the forward-mounted radiator needed to be crossed over in plan to match up with the existing engine connections as this obviated any "starving" that may have occurred due to positive and negative accelerations of the car.

Fig. 31 *The photograph shows the 'Magic Midget' chassis, completed with Jaguar Engine installed, outside the T & T Running Shed, and appropriately enough a Railton car in the background.*

The car left the Thomson & Taylor workshop for Belgium on 11th September, 1948 almost exactly eleven weeks from the commencement of the work of scheming began, and after a short delay due to bad weather conditions, the flying kilometre Class E record (amongst others) was taken at 173.6 m.p.h.

This was another example of good team-work, which would not have been possible without the initiation of the scheme by Col. Gardner with the concurrence of the Jaguar Co., with the welcome revived co-operation of Walter Hassan and Mr. Ken Taylor throughout, and particularly of the T & T mechanics who worked early and late when required with a cheerful willingness that was always encouraging. It is also right to mention that during the war years and afterwards during the post-war period the drawing office had been expanded by the invaluable presence of— incongruously—a German technician, J. Walker an ex-R.A.F. man, G, Kennaway with Naval associations, and P. Horne an R.A.F. cadet and also a keen apprentice.

The writer would like to conclude by paying tribute to the drivers of the cars, Mr. John Cobb and Col. Gardner, who acted as the final link in the chain of events that led to the successful conclusion of the records described and personally feels that in these austere times when opportunities for driving cars of this record type are extremely rare, that their performances were absolutely beyond praise.

Neither of these two records would have taken place but for the guiding genius of Mr. R. A. Railton where this and earlier work on long and short distance record cars must have had a considerable bearing on the prestige and success of the British Motor Industry.

At about this time we at T & T's were pleased once again to meet with Achille Sampietro at Brooklands when he came up with an arrangement of a Magnetic Clutch suitable for the Leyland Engine. This was duly detailed, progressed and built and forwarded to the Leyland Co. for test when it was found to cope with the designed torque required and functioned perfectly. Unfortunately, due to its weight, problems arose with gear changing and undue loading on the engine rear main bearing—so the scheme was not proceeded with. Sammy had also left at the T & T Brooklands Works a set of centrifugal supercharger parts that had been produced earlier for adaptation to a Railton car. This car already had very good acceleration figures of 0-60 m.p.h. in 10 seconds, but it was thought that with the addition of the blower set, this higher speed version of the car could well be used by the Police Force. The unit was fitted to a Works Railton car and test run on a section of the Railway Straight that had not been interfered with during the War. The test run over a short distance, which was all that was possible, however regrettably soon showed that clutch slip was taking place, which although it also showed that the set was working perfectly, meant that either the clutch facings, or the clutch springs—or both— would have to be modified. This, of course, would mean extra work to make the blower set a viable proposition, in that the gearbox and clutch assembly would have to be removed and modified, and so add to the cost of the conversion. No move was made to suggest that this work should be proceeded with, so again regrettably the scheme was dropped.

Fig. 32 Opposite *Shows the Napier-Railton of Mr. John Cobb and the 'Magic Midget' of Lt. Col. Gardner outside the Thomson & Taylor (Brooklands) Ltd. Workshops.*

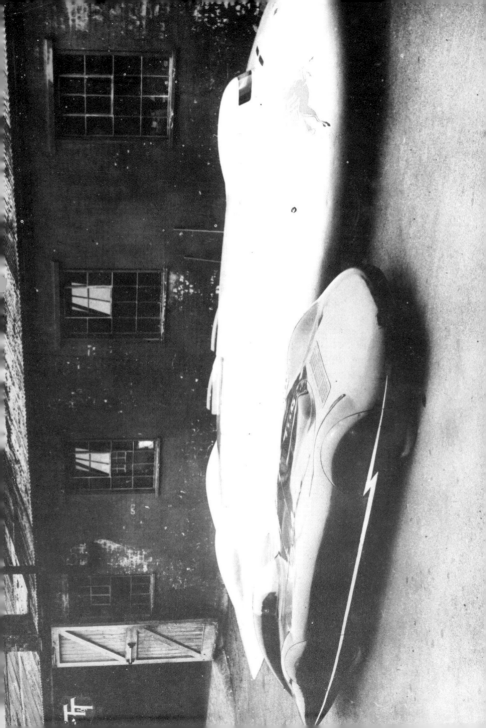

A further suggestion of producing a small Grand Prix car was also turned down on the score of lack of cash support.

Sir Malcolm Campbell had died (through natural causes) on 1st January, 1949 and in the following March of that year we were cheered to learn that his son Donald wished to revive the Blue-Bird boat with which his father had taken the World Water Speed Record at 141.74 m.p.h. as referred to earlier. Investigation was made into the possibilities of using improved fuels, when it was considered that when he had had some experience of high speed travel on water, that the record could be improved to 144 m.p.h. With this in mind the R-R Engine was bench tested and when the power curve had been extrapolated—the bench could not cope with the higher speeds—it was considered that the record was possible. The boat was duly taken to the Lake District when after a very short trial period, one high speed run of 144 m.p.h. was made but only in one direction as the propellor shaft thrust was more that the composite bolted construction of the boat's cross beam could withstand. I was not there at the time but was told afterwards that it was fortunate that his assistants were able to get Donald Campbell out of the boat before it almost sank. The accident was almost certainly caused by corrosion of vital parts over the intervening years and also probably by trimming the costs of preparation. At least it gave the younger Campbell some experience of high speed driving on water, and showed that he had inherited his father's highest qualities.

The naval and car tuning work was still continuing at Brooklands at this time, but it was obvious that the Track would never again be opened as a Race Track, due to the enormous sum that would be required for its restoration or re-build. There was also the possibility that the T & T Workshops would be taken over by the Vickers Co. I believe that this eventually happened. There were one or two nostalgic meetings held at the Track in later years by the Brooklands Society but not attended by myself as my last days at the Track were in July 1949 when I left the firm of Thomson & Taylor (Brooklands) Ltd., to take up a new position, as a member of a team under Sir Roy Fedden in a new Research and Development Division in London, controlled by the Leyland Company.

For me it was an *alpha* of time at the Track with Parry Thomas, of the Leyland Co., and an *omega* of time at the Track with departure to the Research and Development Division of Leyland in London.

Finale

These years at the Track resulted in a great many happy memories and in meeting a number of illustrious personalities, chief amongst them being Mr. John R. Cobb, possibly because he kept his great friend Reid Railton, myself and the whole of the Works with Ken Taylor busy with the two special cars designed by R.A.R. and built by Thomson & Taylor.

The imperturbability of John Cobb has already been mentioned and could be recalled, as on one occasion when the Long Distance Car — already built — was in the Works at the time when the Telecontrol Shock Absorbers were about to be fitted. To investigate properly the room available behind the instrument panel, I had inserted myself upside down in the cockpit and had removed several attaching screws of existing items, when I was called away to answer the telephone. Imagine my astonishment when upon returning to the Shops the Napier-Railton had disappeared! Apparently John Cobb had called unexpectedly to make a trial run on the car, which must have shown up the instability of the instrument panel. Upon his return he mentioned to Ken Taylor, "The instrument panel needs some attention."

As a tribute to John R. Cobb, it is quite possible that a number of class records obtained by him may be broken by other enthusiastic record breakers, but there is one record — that of the Brooklands Track Lap Record of 143.44 m.p.h. — held by John Cobb with the Napier-Railton that is unlikely to be broken by anyone.

The quality of this record may be judged by the fact that it was taken in 1935 (four years before the Brooklands Track closed) in wet track conditions, which may have been of assistance to the car tyres but could hardly have assisted its directional stability.

It seems a very fitting memorial to John R. Cobb that this record should be held by him in perpetuity.

There were other remembered personalities at the Track such as Divot, Dutoit, Segrave and Senechal, with his waving hands off driving after a bend, of the Talbot team; of Prince Bira with his immaculate ERAs; of Jack Barclay's—involuntary and without pause—right about turn at some 100 m.p.h on the Byfleet Banking; of the impeccable driving of women such as Miss Hall, Kay Petre, Mrs. Thomas, Miss S. Turner, Mrs. Wisdom (in alphabetical order!) and others who were I suppose some of the first women to institute the Women's Liberation Movement, and not previously mentioned.

Also not previously mentioned were women members of the T & T Staff—important members, without whom the Company would not have progressed so smoothly. Starting with Miss V. Larkins—Ken Thomson's private secretary—who not only found time to act in this capacity, but also capably managed to cope with the Accounting side of the Company, as well as running a small subsidiary Company by acting as a Co-Director. She was ably supported, as time went on by Miss Thompson, Miss Gowans, Miss Durant, Miss Green and Miss Tanner—all of whom seemed quite able to double as General Secretaries, Order Clerks, or Telephone Operators as required, as well as supplying tea at appropriate intervals. During the War Period Miss Hancocks was an invaluable member, acting as liaison between Jock Pullen and—to Jock—the unaccustomed use of female labour in the Workshops.

Altogether a cheerful and hard working coterie of women who added considerably to the effectiveness of the T & T Company at Brooklands.

For myself I could be nothing but grateful that Mr. H. F. Locke King had had the courage to go ahead and build the Track as I found it a marvellous area in which to be employed, with its spring clean sweep of air across the Aerodrome; with the shallow pools of the River Wey providing a cooling-off plunge, at lunch times, in the hot summer days; with the scent of pine trees and bracken and Castrol 'R' on Meeting Days in the autumn; and with the sight of swans coming in from the Thames and landing on the ice of the sewage farm in winter with wings as brakes and webbed feet as landing gear. With the kindness of Mrs. Railton in providing Napier green curtains to furnish the Drawing Office with a homely touch, and not to object to scissors being borrowed when models were required to be made. Mr. Railton himself summed up the period when in one of his last letters to me he said, "What a good team you and I and T & T made. We had a lot of fun."

A list of the races and records achieved by Parry Thomas, Sir Malcolm Campbell and Mr. John Cobb during this period is too numerous to be shown here, but it seems right that an Appendix should show the many World Speed Records obtained by those drivers as a result of work done at the comparatively small group of workshops in the south-west corner of the famous Brooklands Track.

Appendix 1

The following is a list of World Land Speed Records emanating from Brooklands Track during the period of the book. The first two being designed as well as driven by J. G. Parry-Thomas and built by the Thomas Inventions Development Co. at Brooklands. The remainder were designed by Mr. R. A. Railton with drivers shown and built by Thomson & Taylor (Brooklands) Ltd. also at Brooklands.

DATE	DRIVER	CAR	VENUE	SPEED M.P.H.
27.4.1926	J. G. Parry-Thomas	'Babs'	Pendine	169.3
28.4.1926	J. G. Parry-Thomas	'Babs'	Pendine	171.0
19.2.1928	Sir Malcolm Campbell	'Blue Bird'	Daytona	206.9
5.2.1931	Sir Malcolm Campbell	'Blue Bird'	Daytona	246.0
24.2.1932	Sir Malcolm Campbell	'Blue Bird'	Daytona	253.9
22.2.1933	Sir Malcolm Campbell	'Blue Bird'	Daytona	272.4
7.3.1935	Sir Malcolm Campbell	'Blue Bird'	Daytona	276.8
3.9.1935	Sir Malcolm Campbell	'Blue Bird'	Bonneville	301.1
15.9.1938	John R. Cobb	Napier-Railton	Bonneville	350.2
23.8.1939	John R. Cobb	Napier-Railton	Bonneville	369.7
16.9.1947	John R. Cobb	Napier-Railton	Bonneville	394.2

Regettably, Mr. Railton died in 1977 at the age of eighty-two. His expertise in the design field of high speed cars and boats was undoubtedly remarkable. The brightness of his intellect not only allowed him to perceive the totality of a problem at extraordinary speed, but also allowed him to rapidly find ingenious and successful solutions to them. With this ability coupled to a very dry sense of humour, it is no wonder that a large gap will have appeared in the lives of his family and of his many friends.

Appendix 2
Sheet 1. 3 Sheets

Silencer Regulations
The following is the text of Supplementary Regulation No. 21, which is applicable to all motor vehicles using the Track.

21. EXHAUSTS:—

1. An ordinary touring car or cycle must be fitted with an ordinary touring silencer if and when used on the Track for private and touring purposes as distinct from competitions.

2. Except as above mentioned all cars and motor cycles when running on the Track shall be fitted with the type of silencer hereinafter described.

3. CONSTRUCTION
   (a) A pipe leading from the exhaust valve or valves shall be led into a receiver, which shall be situated as close as possible to the engine.
   (b) This pipe shall penetrate into the receiver to a distance of two inches, and no more.
   (c) The capacity of the receiver mentioned in paragraph (a) shall not be less than six times the volume swept by the piston of one cylinder of the engine, and such receiver if cylindrical shall not be of greater length than four times its maximum diameter and if of irregular shape of equivalent proportions.
   (d) An exit pipe shall lead from the cylinder as far as the back axle. This exit pipe shall protrude into the receiver specified in paragraph (a) to a depth of two inches, and no part of this exit pipe shall be of greater cross-sectional area than the minimum area of the exhaust port of any one cylinder.

(e) The pipes leading into and out of the receiver shall not be opposite each other in the receiver, but shall out of line to the extent of one-and-a-half inches measured at points on the circumference, and not between pip centres, so that if the pipes were continued there would be a space between the pipes at a place where they overlapped sufficient to allow of the passage of a one-and-a-half inch gauge.

(f) No device may be employed in the receiver which would tend to produce a straight through flow of the exhaust gases between the inlet and outlet pipes.

(g) The exhaust gases must not pass direct from the exit pipe to the atmosphere, but must all be finally emitted from what is commonly known as a 'fish tail' on the end of the exit pipe. The orifice of such 'fish tail' shall be approximately rectangular in shape, and of the following dimensions: —
For engines with a capacity up to and including two litres: —
Small dimension — Not more than $\frac{1}{4}$in.
Large dimension — Not less than 6in.
Over two litres: —
Small dimension — Not more than $\frac{1}{2}$in.
Large dimension — Not less than 12in.
The length of the fish tail when fitted shall be measured from the end of the exit pipe to a point situated at the centre of the orifice, and the length of the fish tail shall be equal to the large dimension of the orifice. Thus if the orifice of the fish tail is 9 inches by $\frac{1}{4}$ inch, the distance from the end of the exit pipe (where the tail commences) to the centre of the orifice shall be 9 inches.
The surfaces of the fish tail shall be flattened as far as possible, and shall taper from the end of the exit pipe to the orifice.

(h) The after half of the sides of the fish tail, that is to say the half of the fish tail nearest the orifice, may be perforated with holes not greater than 3/32nds of an inch in diameter. The number of holes is not limited.

4. In spite of the fact that a competitor may have complied with the above Regulations, the Brooklands Automobile Racing Club through its official or duly appointed representative shall

have the right at any time to exclude any vehicle from the Track or grounds within its jurisdiction if in the opinion of such official or representative such vehicle has made or might make undue noise.

5. If while any vehicle is using the track during the progress of a race, record breaking attempt or test, or for any purpose whatever, its silencer should become detached, deranged or broken in such a manner as to allow of the emission of the exhaust gases through any other place than the orifice of the fish tail, such vehicle shall, if competing in any race, record breaking attempt or test, be liable from that moment to be disqualified from taking part in any such event, and shall in any case throttle down and leave the Track forthwith.

6. The Brooklands Automobile Racing Club by its official or duly appointed representative reserves the right to examine the interior of any silencing apparatus fitted on competing vehicles, and may disqualify any competitor whose apparatus in the opinion of such official or representative does not comply with these Regulations, and may withhold, withdraw or deal with as it thinks fit, any prize, certificate or other award to which such competitor would otherwise have become entitled as a result of the use of the offending vehicle.

Acknowledgements

To Ms. Audrey Railton, who kindly made time for helpful comments that led to a very useful contact with: —

Air Commodore F. R. Banks, CB, OBE, (and a number of other international decorations) an established author, who provided his own encouraging advice.

To Mr. H. Mundy of Jaguar Cars for his managerial assistance with "Specials".

To Ian Thomson — son of K. J. Thomson — for his help with photographs and suggestions for promotion of the book.

To Ken Taylor — son of G. H. K. J. Taylor — for his own encouragement.

To John Blunsden of Motor Racing Publications Ltd., for his suggested help with promotion of the book, even before it was published.

To Mr. D. P. Daley and Mr. F. Whiteley of the Mechanical Engineering Publications Ltd. — a Company associated with the Institution of Mechanical Engineers who freely gave advice regarding the manuscript.

To Mr. J. P. Alington a business Consultant from Newquay, who acted as adviser and honorary Solicitor, and to his Secretary, Miss Patricia Mann for her competence in producing the almost final manuscript.

To my eldest brother H. R. Beauchamp — whose financial and other help was invaluable, as was also that of his wife Elizabeth, a Scotswoman, and a successfully published authoress, for her own encouraging assistance.

I doubt whether my English teacher — Miss Couts, would wish to be included in these acknowledgements, but perhaps it would not be amiss to end at last with the School motto of *Finis Coronat Opus.*

4181.
7-2-85.
Regency-Press.